L'Assommoir

A Working Woman's Life

TWAYNE'S MASTERWORK STUDIES

Robert Lecker, General Editor

L'Assommoir

A WORKING WOMAN'S LIFE

Lilian R. Furst

Twayne Publishers • Boston
A Division of G. K. Hall & Co.

L'Assommoir: A Working Woman's Life
Lilian R. Furst

Twayne's Masterwork Studies No. 53
Copyright 1990 by G. K. Hall & Co.
All rights reserved.
Published by Twayne Publishers
A division of G. K. Hall & Co.
70 Lincoln Street, Boston, Massachusetts.

Copyediting supervised by Barbara Sutton.
Book production by Gabrielle B. McDonald.

Typeset in 10/14 Sabon with Cochin display type by Compset, Inc. of
Beverly, Massachusetts

The paper used in this publication meets the minimum requirements of
American National Standard for Information Sciences—Permanence of Paper
for Printed Library Materials, ANSI Z39.48–1984. ∞™

Printed and bound in the United States of America.

Library of Congress Cataloging-in-Publication Data

Furst, Lilian R.
    L'Assommoir : a working woman's life / Lilian R. Furst.
        p.   cm. — (Twayne's masterworks studies ; no. 53)
    Includes bibliographical references.
    1. Zola, Emile, 1840–1902. Assommoir.   2. Working class women in
literature.   I. Title.   II. Series.
PQ2496.F87   1990
843'.8—dc20
                                                                            90-31376
                                                                            CIP

0-8057-9444-1 (alk. paper) 10 9 8 7 6 5 4 3 2 1
0-8057-8132-3 (pbk.: alk. paper) 10 9 8 7 6 5 4 3 2 1

For Dr. Sally Ramsey
A true student and a true friend

Contents

Note on the References and Acknowledgments

All references are given to both an English translation and the French text. The first number in the parentheses after each quotation refers to the most recent English version by Leonard W. Tancock for Penguin Books. Penguin Books has given permission to cite this edition. The second number in the parentheses refers to the French standard edition included in *Les Rougon-Macquart*, vol. 2, edited by Henri Mittérand and published by Gallimard, Paris, in the Bibliothèque de la Pléïade series.

I would like to express my sincere gratitude to the National Endowment for the Humanities for funding, and to all the devoted staff at the National Humanities Center for the support and help they have so willingly given to me: to Kent Mullikin, the acting director, for creating such a civilized atmosphere; to the librarians, Alan Tuttle, Jean Houston, and Rebecca Vargha for providing books on request as if by magic; to Karen Carroll, Maggie Blades, and Linda Morgan for processing words with great expertise and cheerfulness; and last but by no means least to Nan Martin for always having a welcoming word and an encouraging smile. Without this wonderful assistance the task would have been far harder and taken much longer. I am also grateful to the administration of the French National Museums for allowing me to reproduce the Degas and Manet pictures.

ÉMILE ZOLA
Portrait by Édouard Manet.
Courtesy of the Louvre, Paris.

Chronology: Émile Zola's Life and Works

1840	Émile Zola born in Paris on 2 April, the only child of Francesco (François) and Emilie Zola.
1846	The family moves to Aix-en-Provence, where his father designs and builds an acqueduct.
1847	His father dies suddenly of pneumonia. At school Émile makes friends with the painter Paul Cézanne.
1858	Impoverished, Madame Zola and her son return to Paris.
1860	Takes a position as a clerk.
1862	Works first as a clerk and later as head of publicity at Hachette, a major publishing company, where he meets many of the leading literary figures of the time. He moonlights as a journalist.
1863	Marries Alexandrine-Gabrielle Meley, and they move into an apartment of the Left Bank of the Seine, where he will spend the rest of his life.
1864	*Stories for Ninon* (*Contes à Ninon*), a collection of short stories.
1866	First novel, *Claude's Confession* (*La Confession de Claude*). Is invited to stand in for the regular art critic of the journal *L'Événement* and to review the annual art exhibition (*Salon*) in Paris. Writes a fiery attack on the selection committee for choosing dull, traditional paintings in preference to the brilliant, revolutionary works of his friends, the impressionists. He is promptly dismissed.
1867	*Thérèse Raquin,* a novel of adultery, murder, and suicide, which creates a scandal through its outspokenness, is published; Zola defends his practices in the preface to the second edition.
1870	The fall of the Second Empire and the proclamation of the Third Republic.

1871   *The Fortunes of the Rougons* (*La Fortune des Rougon*), the first of a sequence of twenty novels collectively entitled *The Rougon-Macquarts* (*Les Rougon-Macquart*) and subtitled "The Natural and Social History of a Family under the Second Empire." Zola traces the fortunes of the descendants of Adélaïde Rougon in the two branches of her family: her legitimate children on the Rougon side become prosperous middle-class administrators, businessmen, priests, and doctors, while her offspring by her lover, Antoine Macquart, an alcoholic, exist on the margins and in the lower echelons of society. This immense project forms the center of his life for twenty-two years and offers an informal survey of French society between about 1850 and 1870.

1872   *The Kill* (*La Curée*), volume 2 of *The Rougon-Macquarts.*

1873   *Savage Paris* (*Le Ventre de Paris*), volume 3 of *The Rougon-Macquarts.*

1874   *A Priest in the House* (*La Conquête de Plassans*), volume 4 of *The Rougon-Macquarts.*

1875   *The Sin of Father Mouret* (*La Faute de l'abbé Mouret*), volume 5 of *The Rougon-Macquarts.*

1876   *His Excellency* (*Son Excellence Eugène Rougon*), volume 6 of *The Rougon-Macquarts.*

1877   *L'Assommoir,* volume 7 of *The Rougon-Macquarts.* His first big financial success enables him to buy a country house at Médan, where his young disciples congregate. *A Love Affair* (*Une page d'amour*), volume 8 of *The Rougon-Macquarts.*

1880   *Nana,* volume 9 of *The Rougon-Macquarts.* Evenings at Médan (*Les Soirées de Médan*); five short stories about the Franco-Prussian war of 1870, one by Zola and four by members of his circle; "The Experimental Novel" (*Le Roman expérimental*), a collection of five pieces of theoretical literary criticism.

1881   *Naturalism in the Theatre* (*Le Naturalisme au théâtre*); *The Naturalist Novelists* (*Les Romanciers naturalistes*), articles on literary topics.

1882   *Piping Hot* (*Pot-Bouille*), volume 10 of *The Rougon-Macquarts.*

1883   *Ladies' Delight* (*Au Bonheur des Dames*), volume 11 of *The Rougon-Macquarts.*

1884   *Zest for Life* (*La Joie de vivre*), volume 12 of *The Rougon-Macquarts.*

Chronology: Émile Zola's Life and Works

1885   *Germinal*, volume 13 of *The Rougon-Macquarts*.

1886   *The Masterpiece* (*L'Oeuvre*), volume 14 of *The Rougon-Macquarts*.

1887   *Earth* (*La Terre*), volume 15 of *The Rougon-Macquarts*.

1888   *The Dream* (*Le Rêve*), volume 16 of *The Rougon-Macquarts*. Zola falls in love with Jeanne Rozerot, a laundress and seamstress. He installs her in a neighboring house in Médan and eventually has two children by her.

1890   *The Beast in Man* (*La Bête humaine*), volume 17 of *The Rougon-Macquarts*.

1891   *Money* (*L'Argent*), volume 18 of *The Rougon-Macquarts*.

1892   *The Debacle* (*La Débâcle*), volume 19 of *The Rougon-Macquarts*.

1893   *Dr. Pascal* (*Le Docteur Pascal*), volume 20 of *The Rougon-Macquarts*.

1894   *Lourdes*, the first of a trilogy, *The Three Cities* (*Les Trois villes*).

1896   *Rome*, the second of the trilogy.

1898   *Paris*, the third of the trilogy. "I accuse" ("J'accuse"), an open letter to the President of France published on 13 January on the front page of the newspaper *L'Aurore*, accusing the authorities of a cover-up in the Dreyfus affair. Zola takes up the cudgels in behalf of Alfred Dreyfus, an army officer who, Zola and others believe, has been unjustly convicted of treason and sentenced to life imprisonment. For his explosive attack on the army and the government Zola is himself threatened with prison. He flees to England, where he lives miserably for over a year, hating the food and the warm beer. After Dreyfus is cleared in a new trial, Zola is able to return home.

1899   *Fertility* (*Fécondité*), the first of a cycle *The Four Gospels* (*Les Quatre évangiles*).

1901   *Work* (*Travail*), the second in the cycle.

1902   Dies on 29 September under mysterious circumstances, asphyxiated by smoke from a chimney fire in his bedroom. There is still speculation that the chimney was blocked by his defeated opponents in the Dreyfus affair as an act of revenge.

Chapter 1

Historical Context

The action of *L'Assommoir* takes place between 1850 and 1869—that is, during France's Second Empire, which extended from 1852 to 1870. History and fiction are closely intertwined in the *Rougon-Macquart* series since Zola sought to show the fate of different segments of society under this regime. In *L'Assommoir* it is the turn of the working class.

All French men and women were inevitably affected by their country's tumultuous political history in the nineteenth century, when different kinds of governmental organization succeeded one another with considerable rapidity, accompanied by the bloodshed of the insurrections that occurred in 1830, 1848, and 1851. The turbulence is a reflection of the underlying uncertainties persisting in France following the momentous Revolution of 1789, which marks a radical break with the past in the literal beheading of the long-established monarchy. The century following this cataclysmic event represents an attempt to find an acceptable fusion of the principles of the old bureaucratic monarchy, the surviving feudal-aristocratic tradition, and the ideals of liberty, fraternity, and equality proclaimed by the Revolution. These were crucial years in the development of modern France as it struggled

1

not only to evolve its own appropriate form of government, but simultaneously in the economic and social sphere to make the transition from a rural, agrarian system into an urban, industrialized one. It is no exaggeration to say that every French citizen was in some way personally affected by the changes, and forced to make adjustments in his or her life.

The different forms of governmental structure tried in nineteenth-century France reveal the country's continuing search for its identity. After the final defeat and banishment of Napoleon ended the painful period during which all of Europe was involved in ruinous warfare, the French sought a new equilibrium that would have united the stability of the old monarchy with the freedoms of the newer more democratic system. Immediately after the downfall of Napoleon, the Bourbon monarchy was restored following almost a quarter of a century of exile. It lasted from 1814 to 1830, first under Louis XVIII, then under Charles X. Though intended as an experiment in moderation, the restored monarchy finally foundered on internal dissent between extremist factions, which eventually forced the king to abdicate. The next regime, from 1830 to 1848, was also a monarchy, but under Louis-Philippe of Orléans, who as a young man had played a cautious part in the 1789 Revolution and who therefore seemed to offer some hope of compromise. Louis-Philippe's reign was marked by an increasing sobriety and later stagnation as the government's attempts to stabilize a volatile situation produced a rigidity close to petrification. The revolution of 1848, which not only deprived Louis-Philippe of his throne but also destroyed the principle of monarchy in France, was ignited by widespread boredom; irritation at the king's stubbornness at clinging to his old, stale ministers; and practical discontent resulting from the grave economic crisis of 1846–47 when food became scarce and expensive, enterprises closed down, and unemployment rose to alarming heights. The thirst for change led to the institution of the Second Republic (1848–52), which wrote a new constitution that opted for a presidential rather than a parliamentary government. The installation as President of a political adventurer with the name Louis Napoleon Bonaparte seemed to auger the synthesis of the old monarchy and the heritage of the Revolution into a renewed and more promising shape. But after a brief collaboration with the Legislative Assembly, Louis Napoleon turned increasingly authoritarian, and in 1852, with massive support from voters in a plebiscite, he transmuted himself from president to emperor, under the title Napoleon III.

This is the regime under which the *Rougon-Macquart* series is enacted. The Second Empire outlasted any other governmental organization tried in France since the 1789 Revolution. As Napoleon III consolidated his regime, especially after about 1859, it entered into a more liberal phase with a relaxation of controls on the press and public assembly and permission to workers to organize into unions. However, a series of misjudgments in foreign policy left France isolated, and its ill-prepared and poorly led army was no match for the Germans, whose resounding defeat of the French at Sedan in 1870 brought the downfall of the Second Empire.

France's economic development in the nineteenth century was as curious a blend of old and new as was its government. Industrialization began under the Bourbon and Orléaniste monarchies, particularly with public funds allocated to the construction of canals, roads, and railways. Production and trade grew steadily, though not as spectacularly as in other European countries. Because of a tendency to maintain eighteenth-century modes of production and trade and to take advantage of cheap labor in overcrowded rural districts, technological advance was slow and sporadic. In the latter half of the 1840s a severe depression gripped the economy, precipitated by crop failures owing to bad weather and compounded by the confusion attendant on the 1848 political upheaval. This trend was reversed in the opening years of the Second Empire, which coincided with a period of economic vigor characterized by the doubling of industrial production, the trebling of foreign trade, wider application of steam power, and the spread of the railways. But enclaves of old methods of doing business persisted among the more dynamic sectors, hampering progress. By 1862 another serious slump was underway, caused less by specific conditions in France than by a general worldwide slackening after the boom of the 1850s. This is the economic reversal which affects the characters in *L'Assommoir* most directly.

Like so many others, Gervaise has flocked to Paris with Lantier in response to the crisis of the late 1840s when mass unemployment drove workers to migrate from the provinces. This was not an easy transition, because regional differences in speech, culture, and outlook were pronounced. One of the things that *L'Assommoir* shows is how Gervaise gradually acclimatizes to Paris—for worse rather than for better. Her years in Paris overlap with Baron Haussmann's rebuilding of the city in the 1860s, which intensified the social segregation in the city. Different classes used to live in the same buildings, with workers in the garrett and the more affluent on the lower floors (before the days of elevators); the new apartment houses in the heart of the city were far too expensive for the workers, who were driven toward the old outlying areas, where they subsisted in inhuman overcrowding. From her first lodging in the city, Gervaise can see its outer wall from her window, and only once, on her wedding day, does she enter the elegant rebuilt districts, where she feels very ill at ease.

Despite Napoleon III's well intentioned efforts at social reform and liberalization, material conditions hardly improved. The workers were disillusioned, embittered, and frustrated as the mirage of a new utopian era, of which the Second Empire had seemed to some to hold the promise, vanished for the masses trapped in the slums. Told repeatedly that their only remedies were patience and resignation, they were likely to seek more immediate consolations in food and drink (as far as they could afford such amenities), and love-making. In 1864, sixteen years after Marx and Engels's *Communist Manifesto,* the workingmen of the world united into the First International. A delegation of French workers helped to establish it, and by 1870 the French branch of the International was larger than that of any other nation, suggesting perhaps the proportions of the discontent. Certainly, the whole question of the working class was emerging as a major problem of the day.

Marx's call for unity was addressed to the working*men* of the world. Women workers simply did not count in his reckoning although they were beginning to increase in number as a consequence of financial pressures on the family and the changing economic structure. Before the industrial revolution, women had often helped their husbands do their work at home, while taking care of the household and children at the same time. Mechanization sent the men into the factories, and eventually the women perforce too, although many attempted to supplement the family income through home-based cottage industries, such as Gervaise's laundering, where workplace and home coincide. For a woman to be employed outside the home contravened the traditional separation of the spheres, the woman's being firmly the domestic realm of "Kinder, Küche, Kirche" ("children, kitchen, church"), as the German proverb summarized it. Women worked for wages outside the house in the mid-nineteenth century only out of need. Even within the home, a woman's position was ambivalent: as the mistress of the household, responsible for food, cleanliness, child care, nursing, and to some extent money management, she carried considerable responsibilities. On the other hand, she was by law distinctly a second-class citizen, subjugated to her husband in an authoritarian hierarchy. Under the marriage contract, a man owed his wife protection, while the wife owed her husband obedience. Divorce became illegal in France in 1816 and remained so until 1884. Once married, a woman had little choice but to submit, as the law required, and to hope for kindness from her husband.

Chapter 2

The Importance of the Work

Together with *Germinal* (1885), *L'Assommoir* is acknowledged to be Zola's finest work. With it he reached his peak as a novelist, and produced a masterpiece of world literature that is also a landmark in the history of the novel.

L'Assommoir was highly innovative at the time of its publication in its subject matter, its language, and its perspective. The novel gives a vivid and imaginative picture of life in the Parisian slums in the middle of the nineteenth century when population was rapidly shifting from the countryside to the city. Gervaise and Lantier are typical of their period in moving from the small town of Plassans in the south to the capital in search of a better life. This in itself was not an unusual theme in European literature; the young man from the provinces who goes out into the world to seek his fortune was a familiar figure in the novel (e.g., Pip in Dickens's *Great Expectations* [1861], Julien Sorel in Stendhal's *The Red and the Black* [1830, *Le Rouge et le noir*], Rastignac in Balzac's *Old Goriot* [1835, *Le Père Goriot*], and Frédéric in Flaubert's *Sentimental Education* [1869, *L'Education sentimentale*]). What distinguishes *L'Assommoir* is that the central character is a working-class woman, who has come to the city not of her own volition, but in the wake of her man and with two illegitimate children. When Lantier walks out on her (in the first chapter), she is left to cope on her own as best she can. And that is the story of her life, as told in *L'Assommoir*. Unlike such eighteenth-century heroines as Defoe's Moll Flanders (1722) and Prévost's Manon Lescaut (1735), Gervaise is not an adventuress; nor is she an isolated psychopath, like the schizophrenic servant in Jules and Edmond de Goncourt's *Germinie Lacerteux* (1865). She is just an ordinary working-class woman of her time, whose struggles, little triumphs, and big setbacks can be read as an exemplary case. It is significant that Zola originally thought of entitling the novel "The Simple Life of Gervaise Macquart" ("La Simple vie de Gervaise Macquart"). It is, of course, not simple at all, as the narrative gradually shows, but the problems arise less from Gervaise's ambitions, which are quite modest, than from the force of circumstances largely beyond her control. The novel is a fascinating and often heart-rending study of the plight of a kind and decent woman in a foul environment.

Much of the interest and importance of *L'Assommoir* resides in its depiction of environment. Never before had conditions in an urban slum been portrayed with such vigor and candor. Zola aims from the outset, as he says in his preliminary notes, to show how the working class lives and how these squalid and degrading conditions shape their behavior, leading to alcoholism and the breakup of families; how the downward spiral of overwork and under-pay drives workers to desperate measures of self-preservation to escape from their lot. *L'Assommoir* is a document of social history in its picture of Paris in a state of transition during its reconstruction and transformation into a beautifully designed modern city. Meanwhile, however, the workers huddle into overcrowded tenements on the periphery of the city without any share in its splendors. By focusing on one huge house in one limited area, Zola is able to give a broad survey of different trades. The emphasis is always on the everyday and commonplace, even if it is sordid; for the first time in *L'Assommoir,* working-class life is revealed not as the picturesque idyll of romance, but as an unremitting and terrible struggle for survival. To the average reader of its time, the novel was profoundly shocking; to us today it offers a graphic insight into a mid-nineteenth-century working woman's life.

The impact of *L'Assommoir* both then and now stems from its manner of perception and narration. Zola not only chose a modern subject from contemporary lower-class life; he also treated it in an unusually forthright, down-to-earth and direct way. His no-nonsense eschewal of idealization led to a cult of extreme realism. Readers took offense at the unconcealed vulgarities and particularly at the coarseness of the language. Zola defended himself vehemently against accusations of having sullied the working class, maintaining in his preface that the novel is "a purely philological study . . . of very great social and historical interest" (21; 373). His bluntness in incorporating the language of the people was an essential part of his endeavor; he actually sought banality in all its immediacy.

But *L'Assommoir* is not merely an antique to be studied for its significance in literary and social history. Its freshness and energy still come across today. It is a "good read," compelling in the unexpected turns of its strong plot and engrossing in its large cast of well developed characters. Zola's artistic imagination makes people and things come alive; the concrete image of the tenement house and its effect on its inhabitants is one of the most forceful and haunting symbols in world literature. Despite the somberness of the story it tells, *L'Assommoir* exerts a decided magnetism through its original confrontation of the horrors of a working woman's life.

Chapter 3

Critical Reception

L'Assommoir has been from the outset one of Zola's most controversial works, arousing strongly conflicting opinions ranging from the wildly censorious to the highly laudatory.

From his earliest plans for the Rougon-Macquart series Zola wanted to include one novel about the working class. In August 1875 in a letter to his publisher he expresses his great hopes and ambitions for this work, saying that he dreams it will turn out "extraordinary," as indeed it did. At about the same time he already is erecting what he calls "the scaffold" ("l'échafaude") for the novel, outlining the characters, sketching the plot development, collecting documentation, making site visits, and generally fleshing out his project. A good deal is known about Zola's working methods and the genesis of his works because he left extensive preparatory notes, which have been published in French in the fine edition of *Les Rougon-Macquart* edited by Henri Mittérand between 1960 and 1967. Among the seventeen manuscript pages for *L'Assommoir* there is a clear declaration of intention: "To show the plebeian environment, and to explain the people's way of life through this environment; how, in Paris, drunkenness, the dissipation of the family, beatings, submission to all sorts of shame and misery come from the very conditions of working-class existence, from the overwork, the promiscuity, the letting go of things, etc. In short, a very accurate picture of the life of the populace with all its filth, its abandoned ways, its coarse language, etc. . . . A dreadful picture which will hold its own moral."[1]

The novel began to appear, as was customary in the mid-nineteenth century, in serial form in a new journal, *Le Bien public.* Chapters one through six came out in forty-two installments between mid-April and 7 June 1876. Publication was then suspended on the tactful grounds that the author needed more time to complete the writing. This seems a specious excuse, however, since chapters seven through twelve appeared in another journal, *La République des lettres,* in twenty-six parts between 9 July 1876 and January 1877. Most likely, *Le Bien public* yielded to the pressure of indignation evoked in response to the first half of the novel and backed down out of fear of losing readers, even though the editor had cut some of the most daring and offensive passages. This first episode is indicative of *L'Assommoir's* tumultuous history.

In response to the anger stirred by the serial publication, Zola wrote a brief preface to the book version. Under the date 1 January 1877 he defends his novel as "a work of truth, the first novel about the common people which does not tell lies but has the authentic smell of the people" (373).[2] He adds: "Only its form has upset people. They have taken exception to words. My crime is that I have had the literary curiosity to collect the language of the people and pour it into a very carefully wrought mould" (21; 373). This argument represents an attempt on Zola's part to shift the controversy from the question of the morality implicit in the novel to the less charged issue of its language. *L'Assommoir,* Zola claims, "is without doubt the most moral of my books" (21; 373).

The prepublication rumors of scandal surrounding the novel naturally increased its market because of readers' curiosity about the naughty words and scenes. *L'Assommoir* came out in a single volume in March 1877; demand for it was so intense that even before its appearance it had run into its fifth printing. In 1877 alone there were thirty-eight printings, with twelve more the following year. In fact, Zola's masterpiece marks a milestone in printing history too, inaugurating large printings for popular books. The publicity that it received in the press through the scandalized reactions of some reviewers was so great that by 1881 it was into its ninety-first printing. An illustrated edition was published in 1878. Between 1877 and 1879 no fewer than four parodies were circulating, a sure indication of the enormous impact *L'Assommoir* was making. It was performed as a play in five acts on 18 January 1879, adapted for the stage by William Busnach and Octave Gastineau. And when the Irish novelist George Moore went to a fancy-dress ball in Paris in the early 1880's, he dressed up as Coupeau. So the novel rapidly became not just a topic for discussion, but a kind of myth in its own day.

Many of the early reviews[3] are critical to the point of open hostility. In the influential and prestigious newspaper *Le Figaro* of 1 September 1876—even before full publication of the novel—Albert Millaud asserts that *L'Assommoir* is not realism but dirt, not crudeness but pornography. Three weeks later in *Le Gaulois* Bernard de Foucauld reiterates the accusation: the novel is alleged to be the most complete known collection of vileness without compensation, without correction and without shame; readers are spared not a single drunken vomit until they exclaim, "It stinks here!" Henry Houssaye, in the *Journal des débats* of 14 March 1877, would assign Zola's work to pathology rather than to literature, while others dismiss it outright as barroom literature, disgusting, abominable, sickening dirt, one huge indigestion. Because of the obscenity of its language and the immorality of the situations and characters, *L'Assommoir* was denied permission for sale at railroad bookstalls. For a time, because of the French authorities' concern about public morality, the possibility of publishing in Belgium was considered.

However, the reviews are by no means unanimously negative. Albert Dancourt in the *Gazette de France* of 19 April 1876 sees Zola as a mixture of an absolute realist and a striking lyricist, and recommends that the novel be read, but not left lying about afterwards. Although Zola may deserve reproach for the language he uses, he has at least the virtue of frankness, and the conditions of working-class life certainly warrant a blush. Even the forcefulness of the language is praised by Albert Wolff in a further review in *Le Figaro* of 5 February 1877, where *L'Assommoir* is deemed not merely a novel but a revelation, while Zola himself is described as an energetic sculptor who shows delicacy in his roughness.

The most complimentary reviews come from Zola's fellow writers, who are able to appreciate the audacity of his enterprise. Anatole France, in his article in *Le Temps* on 27 June 1877, thinks the book more powerful than likable yet pays homage to the authenticity of its portrayal of working-class life and of its language. Gustave Flaubert, in a letter of 19 February 1877 to Madame Roger des Genettes, finds the novel too long and hopes there will not be many like it; he recognizes, however, that it is brilliant in parts, incontestably true, and likely to be a great success. A sensitive response comes from one of Zola's young disciples, the novelist Joris-Karl Huysmans, who, in a letter to Zola of 7 February 1877, expresses his strong admiration for the beauty of many scenes, notably Lalie's death and Gervaise on the streets. Huysmans published a series of laudatory articles in a Belgian newspaper, *L'Actualité,* in March 1877 and had them issued as a pamphlet in Paris. Another member of Zola's group, Léon Hennique, delivered a public lecture in defense of *L'Assommoir* in January 1877. In an unpublished letter of 2 February 1877, the writer Paul Bourget assures Zola that this is his best novel, and that he has invented a manner. The ultimate accolade is bestowed by the poet Stéphane Mallarmé in a letter of 3 February 1877 in which he envisages *L'Assommoir* as the incarnation of the modern, and declares that truth has become the popular form of beauty. Unfortunately, the more favorable notices are mostly contained in private letters, whereas the negative assessments are in published reviews.

Nevertheless, neither in the short nor in the long run were the adverse reviews damaging to the book's popular reception. *L'Assommoir* was a tremendous success. Zola became acknowledged, alongside Victor Hugo, as the leading French novelist of the period. The huge sales enabled Zola to renegotiate his contract with his publisher and gave him the financial independence to rid himself of the pressures of journalism and devote his energy to further volumes in the series. His other novels also began to sell well as a result of the publicity about *L'Assommoir*.

The fact that *L'Assommoir* is about the working class may have contributed to its success in more ways than one. Readers' appetites were whetted by the aura of scandal as well as by a natural curiosity about an environment not personally known to most of them. It was the middle class who made up the main audience for novels in the nineteenth century. They welcomed *L'Assommoir* all the more because here for the first time Zola's attention was directed elsewhere. The earlier novels in the Rougon-Macquart sequence had focused on the middle class. Now that the bourgeoisie was not the object of scrutiny, its members could delight in Zola's exposure of nastiness. Admittedly, alcoholism was a continuing problem not confined to the plebeian world, but the middle class evidently preferred to see it treated in a working-class context—and they bought the book. In 1881 the hundred thousandth copy was sold. On the other hand, readers from the working class tended to respond with an indignant refusal to recognize themselves in the unflattering portrait represented by the novel.

The commotion following the publication of *L'Assommoir* subsided during the subsequent decades, as the underlying political issues lost their immediate sting. Right-wing critics perceived the abominable conditions of working class existence as the inevitable product of the republican regime, while those on the left accused Zola of insulting the common people. With the increasing distance from the period of the novel, the political strife receded into the background. The tendency to judge the worth of a literary work of art by moral standards gradually came to be recognized as a misguided approach. With the passage of the years, too, the language lost some of its shock effect. Nothing in language changes as rapidly as slang; the vicious terms of Zola's day are, to some extent at least, attenuated through unfamiliarity. Standards of moral expectation also altered, so that no reader nowadays would complain of the smell of the sewer emanating from *L'Assommoir*.

After Zola's death in 1902, interest in his work waned. The newer literary trends of the early twentieth century—Symbolism, Expressionism, Dadaism—cultivated shorter, aleatory forms in preference to the massive novels of the nineteenth century. These movements emphasized the fantastic, the inspirational in writing, not affinities to reality. But through all the successive literary tendencies, a good steady market persisted for *L'Assommoir* because the public at large found it eminently readable; among Zola's wide-ranging opus it continued to be one of the favorites, judging by the number of reprintings. Zola was accepted, with Stendhal, Balzac, and Flaubert, as one of France's major nineteenth-century novelists, although he was sometimes compared unfavorably to Flaubert, whose output was much smaller and whose language and style is choice. However grudging critics were toward Zola, none could deny the force of his coherent vision of France. There was little celebration of his centennial in 1940. The only significant article provoked by that occasion is Georg Lukács's "The Zola Centenary,"[4] which remains the best-known Marxist assessment.

A renewal of critical interest in Zola, and more important, a change of attitude toward him began in 1952 with the fiftieth anniversary of his death. This provided the occasion for a certain detached reassessment. Perhaps it was not by chance that two modest looking but highly important critical studies of Zola appeared in 1952. The first, by the French critic Guy Robert, is *Émile Zola: General Principles and Characteristics of His Work*.[5] Its first four chapters are fairly conventional: a little biography, some exposition of the theories of naturalism, and comment on Zola's method of collecting material and on his picture of the Second Empire. It is the last three chapters that inaugurate a wholly new perception of Zola through the analysis of features largely neglected until then: the mythical aspects of the *The Rougon-Macquarts*, Zola's artistry as a novelist, and his shift from rationalistic naturalism to a visionary messianism. Instead of reading Zola literally, Robert looks closely at the text of the novels, and what he finds far surpasses documentation and social history. He discovers a novelist with a potent imagination, the capacity to transform actuality into telling images, and the eloquence to use words poetically for their evocative resonance. In short, attention is finally focused on Zola's achievements as an artist, not on his role as a moralist or a political publicist.

The second, the English equivalent to Robert's book, is Angus Wilson's brief and penetrating *Émile Zola: An Introductory Study of His Novels*.[6] Himself a novelist, Wilson shows a discerning appreciation of Zola's qualities as a writer. Partly in response to Wilson's book, Lionel Trilling published an essay "In Defense of Zola" in 1953, in which he twice applies the word "genius" to him and suggests his affinities with artists and poets as diverse as Breughel and Bosch, Ben Johnson, Baudelaire, and James Joyce.[7] Trilling is the first to realize that Zola's formulated theory of the naturalist novel is a misrepresentation of his actual method, and to plead that critical justice can be obtained for him only through an unprejudiced reading of his masterpiece novels.

In the past forty years reading Zola has become less controversial and more exciting. The magnificently produced and carefully annotated edition of *Les Rougon-Macquart* has become the standard edition and an indispensable scholarly tool. British and American critics, less inhibited perhaps by inherited French prejudices, have been in the forefront of Zola scholarship. F. W. J. Hemmings has produced no fewer than three informative and insightful books about Zola's life, works, and period. In *Émile Zola*, after giving a lively account of the genesis of *L'Assommoir,* Hemmings comments that "we watch, . . . things of brick and metal starting into a species of independent sub-life and groping with deadly tentacles after the living whom they dwarf and devour."[8] This shows the same appreciation of the imaginative facets of Zola's work as Guy Robert. Harry Levin in *The Gates of Horn* offers a brilliant, concise study of Zola, succinctly relating him to his age and vividly evoking how "he often leapt to the stars from the springboard of exact observation."[9] The many new directions explored by literary criticism in the past two decades have introduced a welcome diversity of approach to Zola. The methods of structural semantics, anthropology, stylistics, and psychoanalysis have been brought to bear on such fundamental patterns as the myth of origins, the tension between the individual and the crowd, and the motif of the scapegoat.

The vast proliferation of Zola scholarship makes it very difficult to engage in any useful survey. Between 1952 and 1980 alone some 2,700 books and articles about Zola appeared. The "Zola Research Program" at the University of Toronto has become the center for bibliographic and editorial endeavors. A vast treasure-trove of letters, manuscripts, offprints, newspapers and journals, photographs, portraits, and caricatures is being collected there. Zola's correspondence is appearing in a series of meticulously edited volumes. *Les Cahiers naturalistes,* a special journal devoted to Zola and naturalism, has been published since 1955 and updates David Baguley's two-volume bibliography for the years after 1980.

L'Assommoir played an important role too in the spread of Zola's fame beyond France. It came to the attention of the English public when the aesthete-poet Algernon Swinburne wrote a "Note on a Question of the Hour" in the *Atheneum* of 16 June 1877 to express his sense of moral outrage at the novel. More favorable publicity came from George Moore, who records in his *Confessions of a Young Man* (1880) his conversion to Zola's theories during a visit to Paris. Moore became a passionate advocate of Zola's in cooperation with British publisher Henry Vizetelly. In 1885 Vizetelly brought out translations of *L'Assommoir* and of one of the following novels in the series, *Nana,* the story of Gervaise's daughter. Though greeted with hostile criticism from the press, they were in such wide demand that Vizetelly brought out fifteen more Zola novels in various inexpensive, illustrated one-volume editions in the next four years. This enterprise formed a part of the attempt to break the monopoly of private circulating libraries, which issued novels in three volumes and exerted control and moral censorship over the publishing industry in Great Britain. Zola's novels aroused great outrage and were condemned as "only fit for swine" in a debate in the British Parliament in 1888. As a result of campaigns by the National Vigilance Association against "Pernicious Literature," Vizetelly was indicted twice for trafficking in pornographic literature, and on the second occasion imprisoned for three months. Drastically expurgated translations were then prepared, although the French originals could be read without cuts in Britain. In 1879 a dramatized version of *L'Assommoir* was performed in London in a watered-down form. Even otherwise astute critics were resistant to Zola: George Saintsbury, who was generally understanding of French literature, branded him in an article in the *Fortnightly Review* of January 1888 as "the dirt compeller," called his works obscene and his methods of documentation "wearisome nonsense." Havelock Ellis, in his study "Zola: The Man and His Work," published in the *Savoy* in 1896, was dubious about Zola's choice of materials and considered him a poor psychologist, but appreciated both his courage and his irony. When Zola visited England in 1893, he was accorded a warm welcome despite ongoing denunciations of his work. As in France, the reading public took to Zola even while the critics were denigrating him.

This pattern was repeated in the United States. *L'Assommoir* appeared in Philadelphia in 1879 in an American translation by Mary Neal Sherwood working under the pseudonym John Stirling. The title page carries a long blurb, in which the novel is praised as "full of nature and of art." The preface offers some biographical information about Zola; more important, it also tries to explain the novel's title by translating it as "The Loaded Bludgeon," then adding that the original has been retained because it is too subtle to be translated adequately. The title has indeed been a great stumbling block for translators, with the result that the novel can be found in English under a confusing variety of titles: *L'Assommoir, The "Assommoir," The Dram Shop, Drink, Gervaise, The Gin Palace*.[10] The 1879 American translation departs significantly from the French text in a number of ways. Each of the thirteen chapters is given a title (e.g., "Gervaise," "A Marriage of the People," "Disasters and Changes"), presumably for ease of reading. The total length is cut almost by half through the elimination of descriptions of the city and details of the work techniques of Gervaise, Goujet, and the chain-makers; obviously, such drastic cuts impoverish the novel. Above all, however, the translation is sanitized, banishing all disagreeable smells as well as other unpleasing features, such as the grave-digger, Bazouge. As the preface states, it is "toned down with literary ability, combined with tact, delicacy and refinement to suit the American reading public." An adapted, expanded translation of the play was performed in New York from 30 April to 17 May 1879 to mixed reviews, predominantly negative. The novel, on the other hand, sold very well. Some readers, whose expectations had been aroused by reports of its shocking content, were disappointed at its relative mildness. But the moral issue remained to the fore, as in France and England: "We would as soon," declared *Harper's New Monthly Magazine* of July 1879, "introduce the small pox into our homes as permit this unclean volume to come in contact with the pure-minded maidens and ingenuous youth who form their chiefest ornament."

It was not until the early 1890s that more appreciative criticism of Zola appeared in English. The voice was that of Edmund Gosse, whose two articles appeared in the American journal *Forum* in 1890 and in the British *National Review* of April 1892. Gosse acknowledged Zola as "one of the leading men of genius in the second half of the nineteenth century, one of the strongest novelists in the world" who gives "a large, competent, and profound view of the movement of life." A hundred years later Gosse's judgment still holds true.

A Reading

Chapter 4

Documentation

"I say what I see" ("Je dis ce que je vois"), Zola maintains in a letter to the critic Albert Millaud written in the autumn of 1876 during the serialization of *L'Assommoir*. In part, this statement is a defense against attacks already being levelled at his novel. Beyond that, however, it also represents a declaration of Zola's artistic creed and of his method as a writer.

"Truth" ("vérité") is a central, repeated watchword for Zola throughout his correspondence and his theoretical writings. It even forms the title of his last novel as though this were the main message he wanted to leave to posterity. It is hard to define exactly what Zola means by "truth"; he is certainly not a philosopher, nor given to anxiety about multiple meanings and possibilities. Like most of his contemporaries, he assumes the existence of a stable reality and a practical truth that squares with ascertainable facts. In that letter to Millaud he contrasts truth with partisanship and propaganda, both of which stem from preconceived positions, whereas truth for him is attained through dispassionate observation. In presenting *L'Assommoir* as a work of truth, he is at pains to point out that it has no concealed ideological agenda, party line, or even, except by implication, purpose of social reform. It is a work of art, but of a particular kind in that it portrays life truthfully as it is, or as the artist sees it to be. This concept of the novel is reiterated and developed in Zola's treatise of 1880, "The Experimental Novel" (*Le Roman expérimental*), in which he insists that "the novelist starts out in search of a truth."[11]

Zola's strong emphasis on truth must also be understood within the context of his time. By the mid-nineteenth century realism was established as the dominant mode in both literature and the visual arts. In envisaging the novel as a true and faithful record of human life, Zola is continuing a tradition inaugurated some forty years earlier by Balzac, who asserts in *Old Goriot* (*Le Père Goriot*) that "All is true." To the realists, truth denotes not only psychological veracity and credibility but also faithfulness to actuality. The rapid development of the physical sciences during the mid- to later-nineteenth century put a high premium on accuracy in observation. The invention of photography by Nicéphone Niepce and its perfection by Louis-Jacques-Mandé Daguerre was also an important stimulus, although Zola, like most other artists, protested against the notion that writers "wish to be merely photographers."[12]

In the creation of the novel truth takes the concrete form of documentation. This is especially important for *L'Assommoir* because of Zola's overall aim of showing the fatal decline of a working-class family in the poisonous environment of the Parisian slums. Since the milieu is intended to be not just the setting for the action but its motivation, it is vital to make it as convincing as possible. The success, or failure, of *L'Assommoir* depends to a far greater extent than in most novels on the reader's ability to believe in the effects of the environment on the characters' behavior. The novel's original subtitle was "Novel of Parisian Manners" ("Roman de moeurs parisiennes"), echoing that other famous narrative about a woman's life twenty years before, Gustave Flaubert's *Madame Bovary* (1857), which bears the subtitle, "Provincial Manners" ("Moeurs de province"). In planning *L'Assommoir* Zola must early on have realized two things, that his predominantly middle-class readership would most likely be unfamiliar with the way the world looks at Gervaise's level, and furthermore that he would in all probability be accused of exaggeration. A sound basis in fact was therefore absolutely crucial.

But documentation is not Zola's initial starting point. In grasping its importance for the novel, it is essential not to end by overestimating it and seeing the text solely as a piece of social history. It is, of course, social history, yet the social history comes within the framework of an imaginative, grandiose work of art. Zola proceeds as a novelist, not as a scholar or a social scientist. He begins with a creative idea: a novel about the working class. The primary spark comes from his mind, from his imagination. The documentation is the second stage, where he deliberately seeks out materials from the world around him to give substance to his idea. These materials are incorporated into the narrative in a pattern of modification, arrangement, and, often, intensification to suit the purposes of the fiction. The evolution of the novel is a reciprocal process of cross-fertilization between fact and fiction as the creative idea thrives by being grafted onto the documentation, which in turn is transformed through its role in the fiction.

As soon as he formed the idea for a novel about the populace— around 1868—Zola began to collect suitable materials, at first opportunistically (for instance, a newspaper article about a child's death through beating by her drunken father), later more methodically. He draws his documentation from two distinct sources: his own experiences and texts.

Zola knew exactly what it was like to try to get by in Paris from his own early years there, when he was managing on a meager salary. Since he moved frequently in search of better or cheaper quarters, he saw several different areas of the city. He states later, in answer to a letter about *L'Assommoir*, that he has for a long time lived among the populace, that he has himself been very poor and has witnessed poverty at close quarters so that he can write about it without falsehood. He was uncertain for a while as to which area of the city to choose as the central location for his novel, but eventually settled on Batignolles in the north of Paris, perhaps because his own home at that time was in the vicinity so that he had easy access to it and could refresh and update his memories. During the autumn of 1875 he spent many hours roaming the boulevard de la Chapelle and the rue de la Goutte d'Or. These are names of actual streets still to be found in Paris. "Goutte d'Or," however, also has an ironic undercurrent because its literal meaning is "Drop of Gold," yet it is attached to a street where there was precious little wealth.

In his field survey, like an anthropologist, Zola would watch the movement in the streets and take notes on the houses, the shops, the street scenes, the appearance of the people. He made a number of sketches, which are among his preparatory notes for the novel and are reproduced in the standard French edition: a general schematic plan of the district, showing how the various streets intersect, with the names scribbled in;[13] a larger-scale, more detailed map of the area immediately surrounding the rue de la Goutte d'Or, where the shops that Gervaise frequents are marked, including the baker, the butcher, the coal-merchant, and Old Colombe's bar;[14] and a plan of the big house where Gervaise lives and has her business, which is precisely marked (as are the neighboring shops and the place where her in-laws, the Lorilleux, have their chain-shop in their apartment on the sixth floor).[15] He briefly but vividly noted the geography and atmosphere of the house, recording the layout of the entrance and the courtyard, the disposition of sunlight and shade, the play of colors, the social stratification. Much of this material is subsequently absorbed into the text. These site visits and sketches helped Zola to give concrete substance and a location to his idea of a novel about the working class. The drawings serve a similar function for the reader as an aid to visualization. Zola also endeavored to immerse himself in the life of the populace in practical ways. For instance, he and his wife would sit on benches in the streets to catch the tone of popular conversation. In the summer of 1875 he paid visits to a laundry, a forge, and a gold-chain workshop in order to gain some familiarity with the techniques of these trades. He would observe people at work, and take notes. It is likely that he picked up information about the flower business, in which Gervaise's daughter is trained, from his wife who used to work in that line.

Zola has often been criticized for being hasty and superficial in

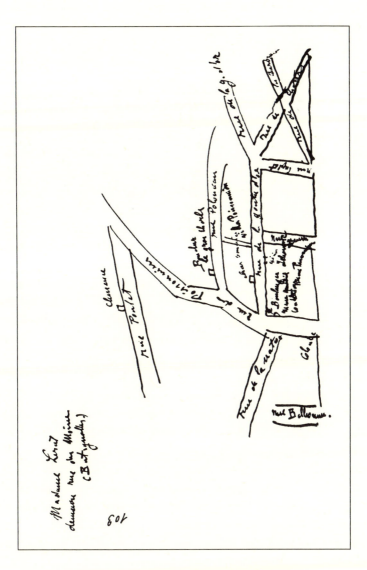

Zola's sketch of the neighborhood around the
rue de la Goutte d'Or.

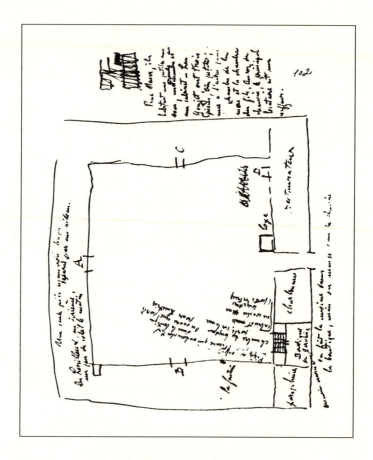

Zola's sketch of the layout of the house.
Gervaise's store is to the left of the entrance.

his collection of documentation. He certainly had neither deep nor extensive knowledge of the trades he presents in *L'Assommoir*. Yet he was quick and enterprising; he had the good reporter's faculty for seizing the essentials, which he could then use by interweaving fact into the fiction he was creating. Zola was, after all, writing not a treatise but a novel; there must be enough documentation to persuade readers of the novel's truthfulness, but not so much as to exhaust and bore them. His documentation corresponds roughly to the preliminary sketches in the artist's notebook. It gives him an accurate basis on which he then elaborates freely, adding and inventing to serve the purposes of his narrative but doing so onto a substratum of factuality. For example, the color of the effluent from the dye establishment in the tenement house is in the course of the narrative pink, blue, pale green, and later black. Did Zola really see these colors on successive visits? or did he invent this as a symbolic denotation of the change from hope to gloom in Gervaise's life? Either possibility is credible, and we shall never know. Nor does it matter ultimately to determine exactly where documentation ends and imagination takes over. The two interface in *L'Assommoir*; Zola the social scientist is not separable from Zola the creative artist.

Apart from such firsthand personal experience, Zola derived information from a large variety of printed sources. Some of it reached him by chance, but most of it he sought out deliberately. In the former category is an account by Louis Ratisbonne of the brutal beating to death of a child by her sadistic, intoxicated father, which Zola came across in the journal *L'Evénement*. As early as 1868, already with his novel on the working class in mind, Zola clipped the article, which eventually developed into the episode of Lalie Bijard, the saintly little mother to her younger brother and sister, who dies at age twelve of exhaustion and abuse by her father. This is a good example of the way in which documentation serves as a springboard for Zola's imagination and for the transformation of fact into fiction.

Zola consulted an amazing range of books in his efforts to grasp the dynamics and the specifics of working class life. He browsed in manuals on the work of laundresses, roofers, chain-makers, florists, and blacksmiths. These supplemented the notes he had himself made in the workshops by providing details about, for instance, tariffs for washing and ironing, techniques of ironing, wages of laundresses and ironers, and rules and customs in washing establishments. In addition to these specialized fields, the more fundamental issue of the present and future condition of the working class was opened up to Zola through the book *A Social Question: The Sublime or the Laborer, as He Is in 1870 and as He Could Be* (*Question sociale—Le Sublime ou le Travailleur, comme il est en 1870 et ce qu'il peut être*). Written by Denis Poulot, a former workman who had become an industrialist, it proposes in its second part idealistic means for reform through cooperative syndicates of employers and employees, education of the populace, and mutual benefit associations. What interests Zola most in this tract, however, is its first part, where Poulot offers graphic characterizations of eight types of workers according to their attitudes, their private lives, and their speech. The term "sublime" is an ironic turn of phrase for the shiftless worker, lazy, violent, and drunk. Zola adopts Poulot's classifications in his outlines of Lantier, Coupeau, and Goujet, each of whom fits into a discrete category, but in the novel itself he does not refer to this typology, which forms merely a scaffold. In an article in *Le Gaulois* of 8 February 1870, "A Wolff et à Richard" by Francisque Sarcey, Zola found a more sober description of the daily life of the working class, some of which he incorporates into his novel.

A direct source for *L'Assommoir* is a dictionary of slang, Alfred Delvau's *Dictionary of Off Language: A Comparison of Parisian Slangs* (*Dictionnaire de la langue verte. Argots parisiens comparés*), which dates from 1866 and appeared in a second edition in 1867. Zola extracted a list of 350 words from it, the obscene language which was to arouse such scandal. Zola's motive for drawing on this repertoire is obviously a quest for authenticity. The title word *assommoir* comes from Delvau's *Dictionary*, where it is defined as the name of a wineshop in Belleville, a working-class suburb. From this original denotation it came by extension to be applied to any sleazy bar, where workers drink adulterated liquor. This special sense makes it difficult to translate it into a single English word, quite apart from the fact that it has other significations too, connected with *assommer*, to bludgeon, and hence *l'assommoir* the bludgeon. Technically, it denotes the pole-ax used to stun cattle before slaughter in an abattoir. The only term that might catch something of the double meaning is "the club," insofar as it could refer to both the place for drinking and the instrument for beating, as does the French.

Zola also needed to learn about the course of alcoholism. He made inquiries with several people and was finally directed, in 1875, to Drl Valentin Magnan's *On Alcoholism, on Various Forms of Alcoholic Delirium and Their Treatment* (*De l'alcoolisme, des diverses formes du délire alcoolique et du leur traitement*), which had appeared the previous year. Magnan was one of the foremost medical researchers into an increasingly grave problem in France during the second half of the nineteenth century: that of drunkenness (occasional heavy drinking) and alcoholism (chronic addiction). A striking growth in alcohol production and consumption beginning after 1850 brought new wealth to France, but also an intensified risk of overindulgence on a sporadic or a regular basis. Between 1860–62 and 1865–67 the average annual consumption per adult of pure alcohol rose from 20.7 to 31.5 liters (21.8 to 33.2 quarts). The French custom of daily wine with meals established a precedent within the family of alcohol consumption. However, it was the growing prevalence of distilled spirits, in the form of aperitifs and cheap brandies, taken between meals on an empty stomach, that resulted in the greatest harm. The overproduction of inferior alcohol and, above all, the dissemination of impure industrial alcohol (the consumption of which doubled between 1849 and 1869) was blamed for the aggravation of alcoholism, especially by winegrowers anxious to protect their income. *L'Assommoir* helped to popularize this view since Coupeau starts his decline only when he begins to drink industrial alcohol. The symptoms of the later stages of Coupeau's delirium tremens were derived by Zola from Magnan, whose laboratory experiments in the 1860s had convinced him of the toxicity of distilled alcohol and of its poisonous effects on the central nervous system. From 1867 onward Magnan was director of the major Paris asylum Sainte-Anne, where the fictional Coupeau is hospitalized. There he meticulously catalogued the physical and psychological manifestations of alcoholism, producing a monograph that won a prize awarded by the Academy of Medicine in 1872 for its contribution to the study of alcoholic deliria. His interpretation of the compulsive need to drink as a sign of a hereditary disposition to degeneration, a psychiatric stigma of congenital insanity, dovetailed perfectly with ideas that Zola picked up from other sources.

Dr. Magnan's treatise does not touch on the social sides of alcoholism. Zola was disappointed to find how little research had been done on this vital aspect of the problem. By the 1860s psychiatric medicine, in an attempt to give a biological explanation for mental illness, was beginning to seek hidden causes for alcoholism. The possibility of cultural and social input was also being considered. Many factors in French life and traditions, particularly in the working class, combined to heighten the practical and symbolic importance of alcohol. Bars, such as Old Colombe's in *L'Assommoir,* were like social clubs, where workers could relax with friends in games and conversation. As Patricia Prestwich points out, "At a time when worker housing was often crowded, cold, and dimly lit, the café, with its glittering gas lights, warm stove, and array of multicolored bottles, provided the warmth, variety, and companionship that was often missing at home."[16] These bars were often homes-away-from-home, providing meals for workers unable to return to their homes for lunch (which is the main meal of the day in France), and in some cases lodging for those without a family. Workers developed the habit of dropping in for a drink of coffee or brandy before or after work. This is prominently mentioned in *L'Assommoir*—except that no one drinks coffee! To stand a round of drinks was regarded as a sign of friendship, so that everyone felt obliged to pay his turn. All these conventions foster the regular consumption of alcohol, which could easily run to immoderate proportions under the pressure of sociability and comradeship. The only nondrinker in *L'Assommoir,* Goujet, is very distinctly the loner. Drinking was unquestionably the norm in this culture, where there was a bar at every street corner. But the bar's prominence is a testimony not to the innate vice or immorality of the workers but rather to its significance as a social and, sometimes, also a political forum for working men. Union or socialist meetings might take place there as well as mutual or sports associations, although in *L'Assommoir* the sole purpose is camaraderie and drinking.

Bars were male preserves which women didn't normally frequent, in keeping with the nineteenth-century concept of separate spheres for men and women. On the whole, alcoholism was less widespread among women, although they had easy access to liquor in the course of their daily shopping in groceries, dairies, and bakeries, or through visits to neighbors. Certain female occupations did have a reputation for alcoholism, and laundering was one of them. Nevertheless, in resorting to Old Colombe's bar, especially alone, Gervaise is flouting the conventions. It is interesting to note that she first goes there escorted by Coupeau. Later she roams the bars in search of him, and eventually she is too demoralized to care.

The consumption of alcohol was also encouraged by the belief, strongly current in France at the time, that it had beneficial effects. A deeply rooted connection had long been established particularly between wine and good health: wine was thought to strengthen the manual worker, to stimulate intellectual activity, to warm and to cool, to quench thirst, to nourish, and to ward off disease. The wine producing industry naturally sought, as part of its sales campaign, to further this image of wine as a physical and psychological elixir. Apart from its action as a tonic, it was touted as a narcotic helpful against all kinds of pain. And since alcohol fortified, it was deemed a professional necessity for those engaged in heavy labor and for those working in inclement conditions. For a roofer, such as Coupeau, a certain daily intake of alcohol would have been considered normal in that environment; it is Goujet, the abstainer, who represents the exception. In plying Coupeau with wine during his convalescence, Gervaise is behaving in accordance with the accepted views of the period that this was good for him. (Contemporary publicists for wine were eager to point out that he comes to harm only as a result of the poisonous brews he ingests with his buddies, and not from the wine.) On the basis of Magnan's study and of his own observations in the area, Zola gives a remarkably faithful picture in *L'Assommoir* of the drinking customs of the working class.

One other nonverbal source for *L'Assommoir* should be mentioned: that of the pictorial representations of laundresses and women ironing by the impressionist painter Edgar Degas, whom Zola knew personally. In April 1874 Degas showed his *Blanchisseuse* (*Laundress*) at an exhibition that Zola visited. In the previous year already Degas was making multiple sketches of laundresses at work in various positions. These pictures may well have influenced Zola's choice of profession for his modern working woman.

At the same time as he was collecting material, Zola was developing blueprints for the characters, plot, and scene of *L'Assommoir*. His notes reveal how the project gradually grew in successive stages. For instance, all the characters, even the minor ones, are listed with their occupations, dates of birth, current ages when the action starts in 1850, their appearances, and personal and working histories. Similarly, all the streets are carefully mapped out with a precise record of shops, bars, and restaurants, including their social status in 1875 in a rapidly changing city. Another part of the planning focused on profiles of the various trades to be portrayed, the working surroundings and the tasks involved. Then Zola made a master plan, in which the action of each chapter and its date is marked out. Even at this stage, however, things were open to change; the first full plan of *L'Assommoir* projects twenty-one chapters, whereas the final version has thirteen. A detailed prospectus for each chapter follows; that for chapter 7 comprises a list of the guests, the gifts they bring, the seating plan at the table, the menu, and the songs each one sings at Gervaise's birthday feast. Not surprisingly, after such thorough preparation, once Zola begins to write he makes speedy progress and few corrections.

Although it is first and foremost a fiction, *L'Assommoir* is a valuable and vivid repository of social history. The action is related to the historical period in which the fictive happenings occur—between 1850 and 1869. Since this was the immediate past for readers in Zola's time, they would have been familiar with the political references to an extent that can hardly be expected today. In Zola's plan each chapter bears a date, generally one year, sometimes more, but even without that external guide the novel's time scheme can be worked out from internal markers. The characters' preoccupation with current political issues is one means of alluding to the novel's frame in history. In the opening chapter, for example, Coupeau talks about Bonaparte and about voting for Eugène Sue, a writer and politician who died in 1857. In chapter 4 Coupeau roams the streets during Napoleon III's coup d'état of 1851, enjoying the riots, the barricades, the rifle shots, and the gunpowder. During the wedding festivities (chapter 3), which are held on 29 July 1850, there is discussion of a law passed on 31 May and its effects on the Republican cause. The guests take sides, but, as so often happens in *L'Assommoir,* they are too drunk to make much sense. This is certainly the case at Gervaise's birthday party (chapter 8), where talk of revolutions and republics is blurred by alcoholic stupor. Lantier's views are a hotchpotch of pseudoliberalism, a revelation of his opportunism rather than his convictions. On no occasion do any of the women voice any political views or even participate in the discussion; under the nineteenth-century concept of separate spheres of activity and interest for men and women, politics fell strictly into the male domain. The historical references become fewer in the latter part of the novel; as the Coupeaus decline into poverty and alcoholism, they are more concerned with day-to-day survival and become increasingly intent on their own narrow lives to the exclusion of all else. In chapter 11, one of Coupeau's drinking buddies mentions having seen the emperor in the streets and having noticed how unwell he looked. This would be in the mid-1860s when Napoleon III's foreign policy and failing health were beginning to cause the troubles that led to his downfall in 1870.

The architectural transformation of Paris represents another form of historical reference. In contrast to the political situation, this more domestic aspect is registered largely through Gervaise's eyes. As she wanders through the streets (chapter 11), she sees the demolition in progress, and the replacement of the old hovels with what seem to her monuments: houses with six stories, their facades sculptured like churches, with bright windows hung with curtains, all exhaling an aura of wealth. Gervaise feels disturbed and threatened by all this splendor, dislodged from her accustomed district, which is being gentrified beyond her means. It becomes almost unrecognizable to her, and indeed, when she goes on the streets (chapter 12), she loses her way among the high new luxury houses hastily built next to the remnants of the old slums.

It is for its record of working-class living and working conditions that *L'Assommoir* is most remarkable as a social document. From the very beginning the sordid, squalid circumstances of life at this level are portrayed. Gervaise is first seen in a filthy, dingy room, full of broken furniture. The grease is so thick that it resists her efforts to clean it off, and she does not even have a stove to heat water. After her marriage to Coupeau, with their double income, her standard of living rises measurably for a while. The apartment next to theirs, inhabited by Goujet and his mother, is invariably a model of cleanliness, order, and proper household management. But this is very much the exception in that area. Through their very virtue, which for the Victorians was synonymous with cleanliness, the Goujets are isolated figures. Slovenliness is the rule, partly out of a cult of easygoing attitudes developed as the only way to tolerate the disgusting surroundings, partly because the overcrowding and poverty are so intense as to defy every endeavor at improvement. Neither the Goujets nor the Lorilleux, who maintain a meticulous system in their quarters out of thrift, has to accommodate children. Gervaise has two sons and then a daughter, and in addition, despite lack of space, she takes in her aging mother-in-law, not to mention Lantier as a kind of boarder. And her home is also her business premises.

The insights afforded into workplaces are among the most original aspects of *L'Assommoir*. The opening scene in the washing establishment is one of the most vivid in the novel both as drama, with Gervaise and Virginie engaging in battle with buckets of water and as domestic social history, in showing how washing was done in the days before washing machines. Laundry could be handled in various ways: the prosperous might have a laundress come into their home at regular intervals, say every week, or two weeks, or even once a month if the family was small (standards of hygiene were lower then, and fabrics less washable); or the laundry would be sent out to a professional washing business such as Gervaise runs for a while. The third alternative was for the housewife or one of her servants to do the laundry in a washing establishment, where a fee was paid for the use of the facilities, as in a launderette today. This is the kind of place presented in the first chapter:

> It was an immense shed with a flat roof, exposed beams supported by cast-iron pillars, and enclosed by clear glass windows. A wan daylight penetrated the hot steam hanging like a milky fog. Clouds rising here and there spread out and veiled the background in a bluish haze. Everywhere a heavy moisture rained down, laden with the smell of soap, a persistent, stale, dank aroma sharpened at times by a whiff of bleach. A row of women stretched along the washing-boards down each side of the central passage; their arms were bare up to the shoulders, dresses turned down at the neck, skirts caught up, showing their coloured stockings and heavy laced boots. They were all banging furiously, laughing, leaning back to bawl through the din, bending forwards into their washtubs, a foul-mouthed, rough, ungainly-looking lot, sopping wet as though they had been rained on, with red, steaming flesh. All round and underneath them water was slopping about, from pails of hot water being carried along and shot straight at their target, taps of cold water left on and piddling down, splashes from beaters, drips from washing already rinsed, and the pools they were standing in wandered off in streamlets over the uneven flagstones. And amid the shouting, the rhythmical beating, the swishing of the downpour, amid this storm of noise muffled by the damp ceiling, the steam engine over on the right-hand side, white with a fine dew of condensation, chuffed and snorted away without respite, and its dancing flywheel seemed to be regulating the outrageous din. (33–34; 386–87)

The techniques of doing the washing are described too:

> She set about getting the dirt out of things. She spread a shirt over the narrow rubbing-board, bleached, eroded by wear and water, then soaped it, turned it over and soaped the other side. . . . She

took her beater and started banging. . . . All the white things had now been beaten, and jolly hard too! Gervaise put them back into the tub and then took them out separately for a second soaping and scrubbing. Holding the article to the board with one hand she wielded a short scrubbing-brush with the other and got out dirty suds which hung down in long dribbles. (35; 388)

After the whites Gervaise goes on to wash "her coloured things in the hot soapy water she had saved. When she had finished she drew up a trestle and threw all the articles over it, where they dripped bluish puddles on to the floor. Then she began rinsing. Behind her the cold water tap was running into a huge tub fixed to the floor with two wooden bars across the top for putting the washing on. There were two more bars up in the air over which things were put to finish dripping" (38; 391). The customers pay the owner by the hour and buy soap and other supplies from her; they use their own beaters and scrubbing brushes, which they can leave there.

When Gervaise sets up in business independently, the organizational and economic sides of laundering are depicted. The basic techniques are the same as in the washing establishment, but the laundry is also starched, ironed, and delivered to the customer's home. The promptness and beauty of her work are at first great recommendations for Gervaise, but as she declines, so do her punctuality and the quality of her craftsmanship; sometimes clothes are torn or have scorch marks from overheated irons. In the heyday of her prosperity she employs two skilled women and an apprentice, although she herself continues to do some of the most delicate work such as lace collars and cuffs. The trade has its seasonal variations, summer being much brisker because the lightweight and light-colored dresses need more frequent washing. Winter, however, brings the advantage of cozy warmth in the laundry, whereas in summer the heat is stifling. Physically it is hard work, not to mention the nauseating smells from stained underwear. The ironing, too, is demanding since the irons have to be kept completely clean and at the right temperature; the starch must be given time to permeate the cloth, yet not allowed to dry. The heavy irons, heated in a fire, can inflict nasty burns in a moment of carelessness. When Gervaise's business fails, she reverts to being employed as a laundress on a weekly wage, but later she becomes so unreliable that she cannot hold down a regular job and can get only day-by-day employment.

Two other workplaces are depicted in *L'Assommoir*: the gold-chain shop of the Lorilleux, and the bolt and rivet factory where Goujet works. Both are integrated into the plot of the novel when Gervaise pays visits. The Lorilleux live at the end of a long corridor on the sixth floor of the tenement house. Their room is like a tunnel, divided into two compartments by a faded curtain; the front part has a bed pushed under the sloping attic ceiling, a cast-iron stove for heating and cooking, two chairs, a table, and a cupboard that has had to have its cornice sawn off to make it fit into the available space. The back portion is the workshop with a small forge, bellows, a vise, and a shelf cluttered with pliers, shears, and tiny saws (69; 424). As in the old style of manufacture, the wife helps her husband, and they both live and work in the same location. They make several kinds of chain: small-link, heavy chain, watch chain, twisted rope chain, and column-chain, which Lorilleux demonstrates to Gervaise:

> He took the wire prepared by his wife and wound it round a mandrel, a very thin steel rod. Then with a saw he gently cut along the mandrel so that each turn of the wire made a link, which he then soldered. The links were then placed on a big piece of charcoal. He moistened each one with a drop of borax from a broken tumbler beside him and then quickly made them red-hot with the horizontal flame of a blowpipe. Then when he had a hundred or so links done he went back to the close work, leaning on the edge of the *cheville*, a piece of board polished smooth by his hands. He twisted each link with the pliers, bending it in on one side and inserting it into the link above, already in place, and then he opened it again with a pointed tool. This operation was performed with unbroken regularity, link succeeding link so rapidly that the chain gradually lengthened before Gervaise's eyes without her quite seeing how it was done. (71; 426)

In contrast to the women's sphere of the laundry, the bolt and rivet factory is a totally male enterprise. It is perceived through Gervaise's eyes as a frightening sort of cave filled with strange paraphernalia and the noise of clanging iron:

> It was a huge workshop in which at first she couldn't make anything out at all. The fire had died down and the forge only showed a faint glimmer of light in a corner, just enough to keep the deep gloom at bay. Great shadows lurked around. Now and again black masses passed in front of the fire, cutting off this last bit of light—shapes of men of colossal size whose disproportionately huge limbs could be guessed at. . . .
>
> Suddenly the whole scene was lit up. The bellows roared and a jet of white flame leaped up, revealing the great shed, closed in by wood partitions with roughly plastered gaps and corners reinforced by brickwork. Flying coal dust had daubed the shed with greyish soot. Cobwebs hung from the beams like washing put up there to dry, heavy with years of accumulated dirt. Round the walls, on shelves, hanging from nails or just lying about in dark corners, was every kind of old iron—battered implements, huge tools standing about in jagged, dull, hard outlines. The white flame shot up still further, lighting up the beaten earth floor as brightly as the sun and bringing out reflections of silver flecked with gold from the four polished steel anvils firmly set in their blocks. (169; 528)

With the advance of industrialization, more efficient machines are replacing the workmen, whose wages are successively reduced, and who are in constant fear of redundancy.

Customs of work become apparent too from the three young girls: Nana, Gervaise's daughter, and Lalie and Pauline, neighbors' children. Lalie has to take on the housekeeping and the care of her younger brother and sister when she is only eight years old, after her mother's premature death. She assumes these responsibilities as a matter of course and maintains an impeccable household despite her father's ill treatment of her. Compared to her, Nana and Pauline are relatively privileged. After they have taken their first Communions at age thirteen, their parents discuss the choice of work for them. Pauline goes to learn pierced work in gold and silver; Nana is apprenticed in the manufacture of artificial flowers. At this social level, it is assumed that young women will work until marriage or until their first child, and thereafter if necessity dictates, if the husband is disabled or unemployed or dies, or if his wage is inadequate to support the family.

Nana's working conditions are evocatively rendered:

> The Titreville workshop was a large mezzanine room with a huge trestle table occupying all the middle of the floor. Along the four bare walls, papered in a nondescript grey with the plaster showing through the rents, ran shelves cluttered with cardboard boxes, parcels and discarded models slumbering beneath a thick coating of dust. The gas-jet had, so to speak, painted the ceiling with soot. The two windows were so big that as they sat at their worktable the girls could watch the people going by on the pavement opposite. . . .
>
> That morning was stiflingly hot. The girls had let down the venetian blinds, but between the slats they could keep an eye on comings and goings in the street, and at last they settled down to work in a row on either side of the table, at the head of which Madame Lerat sat in state alone. There were eight of them, each one with her paste-pot, pincers and other tools and embossing cushion in front of her. All over the bench was a muddle of wire, reels, cotton wool, green and maroon paper, silk, satin or velvet leaves and petals.
> (346–47; 715–16)

Nana is escorted to and from work by her aunt, but she is soon sufficiently inventive to escape this lax surveillance. Longing for an easier and more glamorous life, she takes up first with an elderly button manufacturer; she runs away from home, and is last seen riding in a carriage with a fine gentleman. She has chosen a career more lucrative than making flowers.

Money is, of course, the crux of many of the problems of the working class. Even a provident worker like Goujet is at the mercy of market pressures that fix wages. When he is suddenly paid less for the same work, he and his mother have to retrench their cost of living. This in turn affects all the merchants in the district; for instance, the Goujets decide they can no longer afford to have their laundry done. Zola shows in this way the economic interdependence of the diverse trades as well as the workers' subjection to factors beyond their control.

The financial difficulties of a working woman emerge starkly from the facts of Gervaise's life. Making ends meet is an unending exigency for her. When Lantier walks out on her at the beginning, she has little or no prospect of supporting herself as a single woman with two small children; a laundress's wages are simply insufficient for a family. Her marriage to Coupeau puts her at relative ease, and even allows her to save enough money to set up in business on her own. When her resources are drained as a result of Coupeau's accident, she accepts the offer of a loan from Goujet, and for a while makes regular repayments. However, Coupeau's growing addiction to drink progressively undermines her capacity to manage, for he works only occasionally and spends all his earnings on liquor. Twice in the course of the narrative Gervaise goes to look for him as he comes out from work in the hope of getting some of his pay out of him for household expenses, but both times he evades her. She runs into several other women trying the same tactic:

> She noticed four or five women mounting guard like herself outside the gates of the roofing works, other poor creatures like herself, no doubt, on the watch to prevent the wages from wafting off to the pub. One of them was a great battle-axe of a woman with a face like a policeman, flattening herself against the wall ready to pounce on her man. A little dark woman, shy and refined-looking, was walking up and down on the other side of the road. Another rather dumpy one had brought her two kids and was hauling them on either side of her, shivering and crying. All of them, Gervaise and her sister sentries, passed and repassed each other, looking covertly at each other but not speaking. A delightful meeting, I don't think! No need to introduce themselves so as to get the picture! They all put up at the same inn, at the sign of Poverty & Co. (389; 760–61)

This little episode makes it apparent how typical Gervaise's situation was.

Such concrete scenes make *L'Assommoir* a graphic document of social history. The working woman's budget is delineated not just in broad generalities but in its daily specifics. The cost of housing, heating, food (and wine!), and clothing are all cited in actual figures, as is the midwife's charge. The expenses for the wedding are enumerated: a sum of forty francs to cover the mass, the gold wedding ring, clothes on credit, the dinner, and the fee at the registry. The rates for laundry are exactly listed among Zola's notes: forty centimes for a sheet; thirty-five for a shirt; ten each for a collar, a tablecloth, and stockings; five each for a handkerchief, a nightcap, an apron, and a napkin. Although it would be extremely difficult to translate the amounts mentioned in the text into today's currency, their very precision lends substantiality to Gervaise's plight. When in dire need she resorts to the pawnbroker for ready cash. Again the dilemma is made to come alive: in an attempt to conceal from the neighbors what she is doing, Gervaise sends her mother-in-law to the pawnshop with the article to be surrendered hidden under her skirts. The facts of social history become memorable through their presentation in *L'Assommoir* in such imaginative incidents.

The scourge of alcoholism, too, is conveyed through sharp illustration. In the opening scene already, as Gervaise watches the workmen streaming into the city at daybreak, she notices some of them slinking off to bars instead of going to work. The drinking dive with its strange distilling machine is the hub of the district, over which it diffuses the smell of liquor. On all her comings and goings Gervaise repeatedly encounters drunks on the streets and even in the workshops. For example, at the bolt and rivet factory she asks a workman for directions: "From his open mouth he breathed fumes of alcohol like the smell from old casks of brandy just broached" (168–69; 527). Each of the big celebrations—the wedding, the birthday—ends in a drunken orgy, although Coupeau and his buddies hardly need any pretext for a drinking spree. As Coupeau's bouts intensify, he disappears for days on end, and Gervaise has to look for him in the bars. The start of her birthday party is delayed by his embarrassing absence, and when he does finally turn up he is in a dangerous mood. Nor is Coupeau an isolated case; alcoholism is shown to be endemic among the working class, and to breed violence. Bijard in his drunken stupor beats first his wife and then his daughter to death. Ultimately the poison catches up with the abusers: Coupeau develops delirium tremens and is hospitalized several times for detoxification, but as soon as he gets home he is back on the bottle. The description of his compulsive jerking jig and his tortured delusions is among the highlights of *L'Assommoir*; it shows the brilliant use that Zola makes of his carefully acquired documentary materials to turn them into an impressive novel.

Chapter 5

An Experiment in Determinism

In the second volume of the standard French edition of *Les Rougon-Macquart*, immediately after *L'Assommoir* there is a double-page foldout depicting the family's genealogical tree.[17] Zola adds a note (799–800), dated 2 April 1878, explaining that he is publishing the tree at this point in response to demand from readers, to help them get their bearings among the numerous members of the family whose story he is telling. The pictorial representation certainly makes the relationships within the family much easier to grasp. Zola maintains in the appended note that this tree has been in existence since 1868, when he began work on the series. Among his notes there are some early versions in the form of a diagram, drawn up in 1869, but at a quite rudimentary stage. It was only in 1878, after the composition of *L'Assommoir* that the family tree really crystallized as the organizing schema informing the entire enterprise. Even then it is not complete. One subsequently important character, Jacques Lantier, the homicidal railroad engineer in *The Human Beast* (1890, *La Bête humaine*), was put in as an afterthought. He is introduced as a third illegitimate son of Gervaise Macquart and Lantier, a brother to Claude and Etienne who appear as children in *L'Assommoir*. The family tree obviously

43

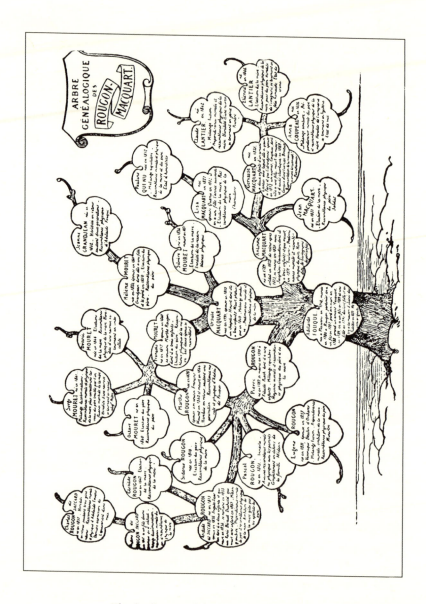

The family tree of the Rougon-Macquarts.

continued to grow as Zola's plans expanded, and he wrote figures in to suit his artistic purposes. The 1878 version comprises twenty-six characters; the final one of 1893, appended to the last novel in the series, *Dr. Pascal* (1893, *Le Docteur Pascal*), contains thirty-two.[18]

These variations in the family tree do not in any way lessen its importance. On the contrary, its history illustrates two significant factors. First, it reveals the ambitious scope of Zola's project to portray the natural and social history of a family under the Second Empire. He ends up tracing its fate through five generations, showing how the family multiplies and proliferates for a time, only to decline and regress in the end. Secondly, the development of the tree indicates clearly that Zola was primarily a creative artist, who invented whatever was necessary to his fiction. The late addition of Jacques Lantier is a striking instance of this freedom of the imagination. To realize this does not invalidate Zola's claims to be working like a scientist. But it does point to the twofold nature of Zola's writing, and it also suggests that he was not always fully aware of his own artistic processes.

The family tree is absolutely central to *The Rougon-Macquarts* series because it is the figural representation of the concept of heredity, which is inherent in the portrayal of a family sequence. In choosing to put heredity at the core of these novels Zola is taking up one of the scientific discoveries of his age. Although there was great interest in heredity in the seventeenth and eighteenth centuries, it was not until 1865 that the Austrian botanist Gregor Mendel (1822–84) formulated the laws of heredity through the crossbreeding of plants. When, therefore, Zola writes in the 1871 preface to *The Fortune of the Rougons* (*La Fortune des Rougon*) the opening volume of the series, that "heredity has its laws, like weight," he is referring to a topic of immediate interest.[19] Mendel's statistical approach was fully accepted by scientists only in the early twentieth century. In the meantime, a great deal of speculation occurred about what was then still largely a mysterious matter. One main question was whether the offspring obtained all its traits directly from its biological parents, or developed according to other, external, influences as well. While most nineteenth-century biologists agreed that some kind of hereditary influence was at play, they differed in the explanations they advanced for the phenomenon, some preferring a physiological orientation, others favoring a psychic one.

Zola's major source of information about heredity was a treatise published by a Dr. Prosper Lucas in two volumes, the first appearing in 1842 with 626 pages and the second in 1850 with 936. Its title is as awesome as its dimensions: *Philosophical and Physiological Treatise on Natural Heredity in the Healthy and the Diseased Nervous System, Together with the Consistent Application of the Laws of Procreation to the General Treatment of the States Engendered by It* (*Traité philosophique et physiologique de l'hérédité naturelle dans les états de santé et de maladie du système nerveux, avec l'application méthodique des lois de la procréation au traitement général des affections dont elle est le principe*). This treatise is a most curious amalgam of scientific hunches and superstitions; some of its hypotheses foreshadow modern theories of heredity, while others are quite grotesque. Zola evidently worked his way through these tomes with genuine zeal. His fascination with the ideas explored by Lucas is demonstrated by the fifty pages of notes he took.[20] He even made further notes on his own notes, outlining for himself how the concept could be used in the novels. For instance, he jots down: "In the novel on the working class, or some other, make a beautiful courtesan be born. In Rome, the most beautiful courtesans come from the populace."[21] This is the seed for Nana. Toward the end of these notes on the notes he lays down, in italics: "There must be hereditary diseases in my work that kill two or three of the characters."[22] The alcoholism in *L'Assommoir* fulfills this bill. Since the notes are fragmentary, it is not easy to construe them in every detail. However, certain things stand out. Zola concurs with Lucas that heredity is "an immense problem"[23] in the social, political and legal sphere as well as in the physiological, and for this reason he accords it more prominence than any previous writer. He insists that "heredity is a *law*, a *force*, and a *fact*" that determines human life at its very source.[24] Everything can be hereditary, not necessarily in itself, but as a tendency; the case in point here is the inclination to drink which is categorically cited.[25] Zola is also struck by the notion put forward by Lucas that the actual circumstances of procreation affect the offspring, so that a mother brutalized during intercourse may transmit the damage to her child, as happens with Gervaise.

However bizarre some of these views may seem to us today, there is no doubt of their formative impact on Zola. In the preface to the first novel of *The Rougon-Macquarts*, just after asserting that "heredity has its laws," Zola refers to his attempt to "trace out the thread which leads mathematically from one man to another."[26] The word "mathematically" alludes to the inevitability of the process: there is no way to escape one's heredity. In *The Rougon-Macquarts* it is a negative burden, stemming from what Zola calls "a first organic lesion."[27] The family's maternal ancestress, Adélaïde Fouqué, whose originating function is shown by her position at the central base of the tree trunk, drifts into insanity and has to be locked up in an asylum. Her descendants on the left side of the tree, fathered by her legal husband, Rougon, who is a gardener by profession, are on the whole right-minded, law-abiding citizens, although occasional reverberations of Adélaïde's imbalance are insinuated (for instance in her granddaughter Marthe Rougon, in whom the heredity surfaces after characteristically jumping a generation). On the right side of the tree the situation is worse: these are the offspring of Adélaïde's liaison with Antoine Macquart, the former soldier in the Napoleonic wars who succumbs to the alcoholism he has inherited from his father. Gervaise is the second child of this unpromising pair. Her caption on the family tree (on the lower right-hand branch) describes her as "Born in 1828, has two children by a lover Lantier with whom she moves to Paris and who abandons her; marries a workman, Coupeau, in 1852, by whom she has a daughter, dies of destitution and alcoholism in 1869. Conceived in drunken state, limps. Imprint from her mother in the moment of conception. Laundress."

This laconic summary of Gervaise's life reveals just how literally Zola took the current theories of heredity. Even more than most of his contemporaries, he was excited by the scientific advances of the time and eager to integrate them into his works. Heredity offered the perfect organizing principle for his broadly conceived survey of French society under the Second Empire. And in fact it does work rather well in *The Rougon-Macquarts,* linking the separate novels together into an organic whole without intruding on the autonomy of any one. In some of its wilder manifestations, Zola's version of heredity may strike today's readers as exaggerated, but by and large it proves a successful schema in which to enframe the series.

The question of heredity is more prominent when *The Rougon-Macquarts* is considered as a series than in the individual novels. Part of the interest lies in seeing the continuities, as in a television serial. Having finished *L'Assommoir,* what reader does not feel curious about the fate of Nana, whose spectacular rise and fall forms the subject of the next novel but one, *Nana* (1880)? To read *Nana* after *L'Assommoir* is to understand her better, because one has insight into her heredity, background, upbringing, and early childhood experiences. Similarly, to read *L'Assommoir* after *The Fortune of the Rougons* is to know where Gervaise comes from. The series is so constructed that it is not necessary to take the novels in sequence, or indeed to read more than one, since each is self-contained. However, the underlying theme of heredity is less evident in the single instance than cumulatively.

In *L'Assommoir* heredity takes the form primarily of alcoholism. Gervaise's father was an alcoholic, and memories of those days have left her with strong feelings. When Coupeau first takes her to Old Colombe's bar, where she smells the fumes of alcohol mingled with pipe smoke, she exclaims spontaneously, "Oh, drinking is beastly!" She recalls how she used to drink anisette with her mother in her youth in Plassans until one day "it nearly did her in, and that had put her off, so that now she couldn't bear the sight of liquor"(55; 410). Yet despite the prejudices engendered by these bad early experiences, Gervaise herself, too, eventually falls prey to alcoholism. This is perhaps a puzzling aspect of the novel, unless Zola's belief in the power of heredity is understood. Gervaise's limp is the physical sign of her origins and heredity. "Even her slight limp she got from the poor woman, whom old Macquart used to thrash the life out of. Her mother had told her a hundred times about nights when her father came home drunk and went in for such brutal love-making that her

limbs were black and blue; and she must have started
nights, with her gammy leg"(54; 408). As Gervaise grows
fatter, and more neglectful of herself, her limp becomes more pronounced. This suggests that her heredity is catching up with her. She
has an ingrained physical and moral predisposition to alcoholism,
which has greater force than her willpower or her conscious desires.
Under the impact of her environment and the pressure of circumstances, surrounded by drinkers and in despair, she gives in to her
innate gross appetite for liquor as well as for food. In other words, the
course of her life is determined by forces beyond her volitional control.

So is Coupeau's. Like Gervaise, he bears a heredity of alcoholism.
His father, who had been a roofer before him, had fallen off a roof
and smashed his head one day when he had been drinking. Coupeau
assures Gervaise before their marriage that this unhappy memory has
kept his entire family sober ever since. Coupeau's own path refutes
this assertion. No more than Gervaise can he escape the tarnish of
inherited alcoholism. When he is in the last stages of delirium tremens
at the hospital, the younger doctor asks Gervaise:

> "Did this man's father drink?"
>
> "Well, Sir, a bit, just like everybody else. . . . He lost his life in a
> fall from a roof one day when he was tight."
>
> "Did the mother drink?"
>
> "Well, of course, Sir, just like everybody else, you know, a drop
> now and again. . . . Oh, but it's a very respectable family. . . . There
> was a brother who died very young of convulsions."
>
> The doctor looked at her with his piercing eyes and went on
> brutally:
>
> "And do you drink too?"
>
> She floundered and protested, put her hand to her heart to pledge
> her sacred word.
>
> "You do! Well, watch out, you see where drink lands you. One
> of these days you'll die in the same way!" (413; 786)

The rising generation of physicians, familiar with the newest findings,
is aware of the implications of both heredity and environment on those
who drink.

In Nana the full effects of heredity will not show until the novel devoted to her story. According to the entry on the family tree she resembles her mother physically and takes after her father morally. Nana gets her good looks from Gervaise, who was an attractive woman in her youth. She also gets from her mother an appetite for goodies, which she doesn't bother to conceal at her mother's birthday feast when she grabs all the best morsels for herself. But her self-seeking viciousness is an intensified replica of her father's behavior. Little attention is given to Gervaise's other two children, Etienne and Claude, although they are the central characters of later novels in the *Rougon-Macquarts* saga, namely *Germinal* (1885) and *The Masterpiece* (1886, *L'Oeuvre*) respectively.

The notion of heredity is only one strand in the theoretical baggage that Zola brought to *L'Assommoir,* and one facet of the novel's deterministic worldview. Determinism is the philosophical doctrine that every event, act, and decision is the inevitable consequence of antecedents, such as physical, psychological, or environmental conditions, that are independent of the human will. Although determinism had earlier been prevalent, it was given significant reinforcement by the scientific discoveries of the nineteenth century. Foremost among these was Charles Darwin's momentous theory of evolution, put forward in 1859 in *On the Origin of Species by Natural Selection.* Working from data collected in the Galápagos Islands, Darwin postulated that man had evolved from the lower species by a very gradual process of adaptation to environment as well as through a natural selection by means of the survival of the fittest. Darwin's revolutionary perception of human beings and their relationship to the world aroused vociferous opposition, particularly from established religious authorities who saw Darwin's scenario as a rival, and a threat, to the biblical story of the creation. Uncomfortable though it was to most Victorians suddenly to have to envisage themselves as descended from apes and jellyfish, Darwin's thesis was sufficiently persuasive to be taken seriously. As an innovative vision it also held great appeal for the imagination. Its message of biological determinism came to be increasingly respected and accepted in the latter half of the nineteenth century. Zola was one of its most enthusiastic exponents and through his novels one of its major popularizers.

The technological advances of the time, such as the development of a railroad network and the introduction of gas lighting on city streets, heightened the prestige of the sciences. The scientific method gained widespread admiration, and was adopted and emulated in the social sciences and the humanities. The French mathematician and philosopher Auguste Comte argued in his *Course on Positivist Philosophy* (1838; 2 ed. 1864, *Cours de philosophie positive*) that science provides the model for the only kind of knowledge human beings can attain. All we know of reality is what we can observe or legitimately deduce from what we observe. This makes everything subject to empirical verification. Comte maintained, too, that all phenomena are interrelated in processes of cause and effect, and that the laws governing these natural chains of events are ascertainable. If event B has constantly been observed to follow event A under certain conditions, then, given exactly the same conditions, we are entitled to suppose that B will again follow A. This is another way of saying by logic what Darwin was showing through empirical observation: that the phenomena of the physical world unfold along a determined and determinable pattern. Great emphasis was placed on, and great faith invested in, the validity of the method itself, which was thought to be transferable to other spheres of life, including the moral and the psychological.

One sphere in which the new scientific method was to prove highly successful was medicine. Claude Bernard's *Introduction to the Study of Experimental Medicine* (1865, *Introduction à l'étude de la médecine expérimentale*) aimed to transform medicine from the intuitive art it had been into a scientific discipline dependent solely on observation and deduction. It takes as its starting point Comte's proposition that physical phenomena repeat themselves according to discoverable patterns.

The new scientific method was eagerly espoused by Zola, who tries in his 1880 treatise "The Experimental Novel" to draw a parallel between the scientist's approach and that of the novelist. Its very title proclaims its indebtedness to Bernard. Zola maintains that the experimental method, which has already been extended from physics and chemistry to physiology and medicine, can equally well be carried over into psychology and the novel:

> We have experimental chemistry and physics; we shall have exper-
> imental physiology; later still we shall have the experimental
> novel. . . . Everything holds together; it was necessary to start with
> the determinism of living bodies; and since scientists like Claude
> Bernard now show that fixed laws govern the human body we can
> assert without fear of mistake that the day will come when the laws
> of thought and the passions will be formulated in their turn. One
> and the same determinism must govern the stone in the road and
> the brain of man.[28]

Indirectly Zola is projecting here in theoretical terms what he sees himself doing in *The Rougon-Macquarts*. He envisages the novelist as a cross between an anatomist and a social scientist, applying the scientific method to the natural and social study of mankind. The novel therefore represents a kind of practical sociology, in which the mechanism of human behavior can be demonstrated and illustrated. Such a concept of the novel is dubious and simplistic. Zola proved far better as a novelist than as a theoretician. But it is important to understand his intentions and the context of his thought from which they arose.

L'Assommoir can therefore be deemed an experiment in determinism, showing how certain people behave under certain circumstances. The three factors that were thought to condition behavior are heredity, environment, and the pressure of the moment. These were designated the crucial determinants by the literary critic Hippolyte Taine in a set of essays written in the early to mid-1860s. A philosophical materialist as well as a proponent of Darwin, Taine contended that the human animal is a continuation of the primitive animal. In both humans and animals the primary molecule is inherited, and its acquired shape passed on partially and gradually by heredity. In both also the molecule develops its configuration under the influence of its environment. To these biological elements, which Taine calls *la race* (heredity) and *le milieu* (environment), he adds *le moment* (the moment, i.e., the pressure of circumstances) to complete the explanation of human behavior. So an individual with a specific heredity, brought up and living in a specific environment, will under the pressure of specific circumstances behave in a predictable manner.

This is the script that is played out in *L'Assommoir*. Heredity is represented in the Rougon-Macquarts' family tree. Environment is drawn from Zola's own early experiences and from his purposeful documentation. Because the environment is assigned so central a function in the motivation of the action, it was essential to convey its feel and atmosphere to readers. More than a century later, to readers who have no prior acquaintance with the setting, the scene of Gervaise's life leaves a lasting impression. Its pungent smells and the depth of its miseries are not likely to be forgotten.

The cardinal role of environment in *L'Assommoir* is spelled out by Zola in the preface: "My characters are not bad, but only ignorant and spoilt by the environment of grinding toil and poverty in which they live" (21; 374). This argument, which shifts responsibility from the individual onto the social situation, can only be fully understood in light of Zola's belief in determinism. That doctrine is at the crux and the core of *L'Assommoir*. While it shapes the path of each of the characters, it is particularly momentous for the women because they have been brought up in the nineteenth century always to conform and to obey, never to resist or to assert themselves. They are thus laid open to insidious outside influences, and the results can be catastrophic. Gervaise herself is aware of this special dilemma of the woman: "It wasn't true that she was strong-minded; on the contrary she was very weak and let herself go wherever she was pushed for fear of upsetting anybody. Her great wish was to live with nice people because, she said, to be with nasty people was like being bashed on the head, it cracked your shell open and did you in if you were a woman" (62; 417). This is one of the passages where the English does not have the same force as the original text. The French phrase, "la mauvaise société . . . ça vous aplatissait une femme en moins de rien" means literally that bad company would lay a woman flat into less than nothing. It has a certain sexual innuendo that is missing in the less ambivalent "did you in."

Environment in *L'Assommoir* has simultaneously a physical and a moral dimension; it consists largely of depressing places and self-seeking people, although there are exceptions, such as Goujet and Lalie. Again, this is particularly destructive for a nineteenth-century woman because she has so little freedom of movement. At Gervaise's social level, conventions were in fact not as restrictive as in the middle or upper classes, where women were guarded and chaperoned for their own protection. On the other hand, Gervaise does not have the financial means to go away. Coupeau gets away to the country for a while during his convalescence, and comes back markedly better. Gervaise never has any break from her daily round of toil, and hardly ever leaves her immediate home area. Fares on the public system of horse-cars were fairly expensive, and Gervaise is further limited by her limp. The only occasion in the novel in which she is seen beyond her district is on the day of her wedding. The hilarious episode of the visit to the museum, where the party loses its way and is afraid of being locked in, very effectively suggests how ill at ease members of the working class are when out of their familiar surroundings.

Those surroundings amount to a form of imprisonment, especially for a woman. By the close of the first chapter, as Gervaise surveys her situation, she realizes "with a dull terror" that "life itself from now on was going to live itself out in this place, between a slaughter-house and a hospital" (49; 403). The choice of buildings is significant: the slaughterhouse is where animals die, and the hospital where human beings were very likely to meet death at that time. From then on *L'Assommoir* is the story of Gervaise's increasing physical and moral confinement, as her dwellings diminish in size and amenity and her options are reduced virtually to nil. Her growing enclosure is expressed, and symbolized, by her actual location. In the opening chapter she sits looking out of a window, although her view is barred on the horizon by the wall surrounding Paris. The more she comes down in the world, the narrower her quarters:

> Just one room and a smaller one, and no more. That was where the Coupeaus roosted now. And even the larger room was no bigger than your hand. You had to do everything in it, sleep, eat and every-

thing else. The little room just held Nana's bed; she had to undress in her parents' room and her door had to be left open at night to give her some air. The place was so small that Gervaise had left some of her things for the Poissons when she gave up the shop because she couldn't get everything in. What with the bed, the table and four chairs, the place was chock-a-block. (306; 672)

At the end she dies in a hole under the stairs.

The physical and moral aspects of environment are embodied in both the tenement house and Old Colombe's bar. Zola's decision to change the title from "The Simple Life of Gervaise Macquart" to *L'Assommoir* indicates a shift of emphasis from the individual onto the group in the orbit of the drinking dive. While Gervaise remains the focus of interest, the novel is also the story of Coupeau, Goujet, and Lalie, and its total import transcends her fate, although her lot is paradigmatic. As the picture widens, the environment gains in importance, and so does the bar. Physically, Old Colombe's is the spot where all the drinkers gather; morally, it is the source of pollution for the whole neighborhood as the demon of alcoholism ravages its victims and their families; and artistically, it is the novel's center of gravity, from which the action opens out in concentric circles. The fumes from the still, as they drift over the area, are through their insistent presence constant reminders of the power that alcohol exerts over the inhabitants. It is the poison that ultimately consumes them.

If the bar is like the inner sanctum of the action, the tenement house is its main forum. The house and the street are, as it were, continuous: smells, such as the goose cooking on Gervaise's birthday, waft out of the house into the street, and so do the sounds of beatings, screams, and quarrels. Gervaise's laundry in particular, being at the front of the house facing the street at ground level, is open to comings and goings. In the summer heat door and windows are thrown open, while in winter people come in to take shelter and enjoy the warmth. This continual interchange between house and street suggests a number of things. On the simplest plane it illustrates very pointedly the individual's lack of privacy in such surroundings. Everybody in the rue de la Goutte d'Or knows everybody else's business and personal problems. When a newcomer arrives, such as Gervaise at the beginning, one of the neighbors quickly finds out her background and situation in conversation at the washing establishment. Privacy, like space, is a privilege of the rich. The poor, on the other hand, live in reciprocal interdependence: economically, when lowered wages in one trade threaten the livelihood in others, and socially, through their need to accept and to give help. Goujet helps Gervaise as best as he can, and she does the same for Lalie, for her mother-in-law, and for pathetic old Bru, to whom she has no obligation beyond the call of her own kindness. Others, such as the Lorilleux, testify to their exceptional meanness by refusing or deliberately withholding humane help to those in need.

This incessant interaction between the individual and the community becomes manifest, too, in the prevalence of gossip. Throughout Gervaise is very keenly conscious of her neighbors' opinions of her. At first she benefits from the widespread approbation of her professional competence and her goodness. Later, however, she is the object of scorn:

> The whole neighbourhood soon knew that Gervaise went over to Lantier every night. Madame Lorilleux's indignation in front of the neighbours was vehement; she pitied her brother, that ninny whose wife deceived him up hill and down dale, and it was understood that the only reason why she still set foot in such a madhouse was for her poor old mother's sake. The whole district fell upon Gervaise. She must have been the one to lead the hatter astray. You could see it in her eyes. Yet, in spite of the ugly stones, that artful dodger Lantier got away with it because he went on with his gentlemanly airs in front of them all, strolling along the pavements reading the paper, full of gallant attentions to the ladies, always giving them sweets or flowers. After all, he was only behaving like a cock among hens, a man's man, and you can't expect him to resist women who throw themselves at him, can you? But there was no excuse for her; she was a disgrace to the rue de la Goutte d'Or. (270–71; 635–36)

The negative feedback from such gossip has, of course, a deleterious effect on Gervaise. The passage is also interesting for showing the differing standards of morality for men and women: Lantier is allowed to get away with his libertinism on the grounds that his conduct is natural to a man, whereas Gervaise is severely censured and rejected by the community. On her daily errands she begins to avoid certain streets because of the debts she has accumulated to merchants, whose stores she does not want to pass. This is a graphic, concrete way to convey the worsening of her relationship to her surroundings. When her mother-in-law dies, she is anxious to do the proper thing, however crippling the cost. In part she is motivated by her own sense of decorum, but this is mixed with concern about what the neighbors will think, as when trips to the pawnshop are concealed as far as possible. The gossip of the district goes on: about Lantier and Virginie, about Gervaise's alleged selling of Nana, about Coupeau's having a permanent cell at the hospital, and so forth. The gossip almost has the function of a chorus, commenting, maliciously, on the action; the district ("le quartier") becomes, in a sense, a persona. This eerily impersonal and ill-definable form of gossip is another way in which the environment exerts a determining influence on the individual.

The environment is always present in *L'Assommoir* in one shape or another: as a whiff of alcohol, as the stench of dirty laundry, as the voices of neighbors raised in discord or whispering tittle-tattle. And nearly always, it carries a negative charge. The physical offensiveness of the odors that assail the senses are a metaphor for the moral unpleasantness that is almost the norm. The tolerance of Lantier's turpitude is an example of the dominant hypocrisy: provided appearances are to some degree kept up, license is extended endlessly. It is Lantier's pose in the style of a gentleman that enables him to carry on his parasitic existence without sanctions. The laxity with which he is treated is symptomatic of the permissive atmosphere of the house and of the district, where leniency is really an expression of corruption. Exposure to such an environment is damaging and demoralizing, especially to a woman's tender ego. Gervaise, fresh from the more innocent countryside, is particularly susceptible to contamination by a poisoned environment. She resists as much as she can, but in the long run she, too, deteriorates and becomes debased. Nana, on the other hand, conditioned to and by this vicious milieu from infancy, adapts to it with a highly developed instinct for self-preservation. She knows exactly how to guard her own interests, and early on acquires a sharp tongue and a foul vocabulary. Her apprenticeship in the flower workshop completes her education in more than one sense. "Oh, of course she had plenty of aptitude, but this was the finishing touch, being with a lot of girls already tainted with poverty and vice. Here they were all on top of each other and decaying together, just like those baskets of apples in which one or two have started to go. Naturally they behaved themselves in public and avoided looking too corrupt in character or too coarse in language, in fact they posed as nice young ladies. But in corners, in whispers, obscenities were rife" (348; 717). As the product of this environment, Nana "took to vice like a duck to water" (351; 720).

Nana is also a good example of the way in which the pressure of momentary circumstances precipitates a particular course of action in a specific personality. From her father she has a heredity of vicious self-interest that makes her put her own pleasure and comfort beyond all other considerations and obligations. The environment in which she has grown up and where she works has reinforced the basic lesson that people must fend for themselves as best they can if they are to survive, let alone to enjoy an easy life, as Nana wants to. The pressure of circumstances comes from the ever worsening conditions in the Coupeau household as Gervaise begins to join her husband at Colombe's bar:

But with the onset of winter life in the Coupeau home became intolerable. Every evening Nana got the strap. When Father was tired of hitting her, Mother would box her ears just by way of showing her how to behave. More often than not there was a general shindy, for as soon as one hit her the other would defend her, so that all three ended up on the floor amid broken crockery. Add to that never enough food and perishing cold. If she bought herself something nice, such as a bow of ribbon or buttons for her cuffs, her parents would confiscate it and turn it into money. She had nothing of her own except her regular ration of blows before creeping between the sheets where she shivered under her little black petticoat, which she

> spread on top of her only coverlet. No, this bloody existence couldn't go on unless she intended to leave her dead body there. (357; 726)

Her parents have gradually forfeited her respect through their drinking and her affection through their abusiveness. Things come to a head one Saturday evening:

> Nana came back and found her father and mother in an abominable state. Coupeau had fallen across the bed and was snoring. Gervaise had flopped in a heap on a chair and was rolling her head with vague, terrifying eyes staring into the void. She had forgotten to warm up the dinner, a bit of left-over stew. An unsnuffed candle lit up the tenement in all its shameful squalor.
>
> "Is that you, kid?" Gervaise babbled. "You wait, your Dad'll give you what for!"
>
> Nana made no answer, but stood there very pale, and looked at the cold stew and the unlaid table, at the dreadful room to which this pair of drunkards added the ghastly horror of their befuddlement. She didn't take off her hat, walked once round the room and then, with set jaws, opened the door again and went out. (358; 727)

Nana's flight is presented here as an instinctive, spontaneous reaction to a crucial 'moment' in the family's history. She has earlier assessed her dilemma in rational comprehension, but when it comes to the point she acts without reflection in direct response to the pressure of circumstances and in accordance with her personality. Whereas a gentler girl, such as Lalie, might have felt pity for her parents, perhaps even a duty to help them, Nana has no illusions and her priorities are clear: to save her own skin. Indeed, she puts the blame on her parents by concluding that they "could just say their *mea culpa* and admit that they had driven her out themselves" (358; 727). Far from feeling any guilt, Nana sees herself as the victim of circumstances. And *L'Assommoir* shows that her ruthless toughness, not Lalie's tender devotion, is what is required to survive in this environment.

Coupeau is in many respects a parallel to his daughter. His conduct after his accident is a precedent for hers so that the workings of heredity are implied in the repetition. Both Coupeau's heredity and his environment impel him toward drink: his father was an alcoholic, and his buddies all drink at Colombe's bar. Yet until the accident Coupeau has been a dependable and sober worker. His fall from the roof and leg injury represent the pressure of momentary circumstances. With heroic devotion and at great financial and physical self-sacrifice, Gervaise nurses him at home, fearing he will pick up some infection and die if he is put into the hospital. In her well-intentioned kindness she spoils and babies him as she seeks to rebuild his strength with succulent dishes accompanied by a glass of red wine. No doubt Coupeau revels in the attention and the respite from dangerous work. No doubt, too, he recalls how his own father was killed in a similar accident. This time he has got off with a broken leg and a fright. He is in no hurry to go back to work, nor does Gervaise in her indulgence press him. On the contrary, she may unconsciously enjoy this new situation, in which she is the family breadwinner and she wins admiration for her goodness toward her husband. At this point in the novel she has more power and more respect from others than at any time before or after, so she may wish to prolong Coupeau's convalescence. But Gervaise is a poor psychologist. She evidently doesn't realize how severely Coupeau's self-confidence has been undermined by his mishap. The longer he delays his return to work, the less likely he is ever to go. As he gets back onto his legs, he takes the short walk to Colombe's bar where he finds company. From wine he moves on to harder liquors and slips into a dependence on alcohol. As with Nana, so in his case the pressure of circumstances does not suddenly become manifest in a single crucial moment, but rather as a slowly cumulative process that leads up to a crisis. Given Coupeau's heredity and environment, the lazing he is encouraged to do after his fall is almost bound to drive him to drink.

In other characters the force of determinism is less easily apparent. For instance, not enough is known about Lantier's background to decide its role in his behavior. The withholding of information about him is certainly deliberate so that he remains something of a mystery. His capital is his carefully calculated air of being a gentleman, a cut above everyone else. He is able to make an impression, especially on women, and to exploit them by bestowing the privilege of his patronage. He is a figure whose motivation and actions are readily comprehensible, although it is not revealed how he came to be the way he is.

Goujet is perhaps the most puzzling, for he alone seems to escape the curse of determinism. He has genes as bad as those of Gervaise and Coupeau, with a father so crazed by drink that he committed murder. Goujet lives in the same environment as they, working alongside men whose breath reeks of liquor. But he remains untainted throughout. Clearly, his mother's presence has a powerful influence over him. Their apartment is always an oasis of immaculate cleanliness in the surrounding filth; they live according to their means, and even have some savings. However, Goujet does pay a price for his purity. He is an isolated figure, an exception, and therefore something of a loner. He does not marry or have children, which means that for him the normal pattern of life's continuities is broken. For all his virtue, Goujet's life is a sterile dead end. His bedroom with its single bed is described as being like a child's. The protective interest he takes in Etienne, Gervaise's elder son, who is apprenticed at the bolt and rivet factory, suggests a father-son relationship, as if Etienne were a surrogate for the child Goujet has never had. So, although Goujet has succeeded in avoiding the more obvious pitfalls latent in his situation, he has not managed to do so without sustaining some compensatory damage.

Zola's experiment in determinism in *L'Assommoir* implicitly raises the question of free will. If personality is shaped by heredity and environment so that it reacts in a certain predictable way to the pressure of circumstances, how much freedom of choice is left to the individual? Does such a view of human life not belittle, or even dismiss, willpower, and so strip the individual of autonomy in the decision-making process? Zola has been described as "a behaviorist who concentrates on material forces and conditioned reflexes. Preoccupied less with his characters than with their characteristics, he is finally interested less in temperament than in milieu."[29] It would be fairer to say that he is interested above all in temperament as the product of milieu.

The accusation of behaviorism—for it does often come across as an accusation—is important because it is related to another charge often made against Zola: that his novels make depressing reading. It would be futile to deny that the conditions described in *L'Assommoir* and Gervaise's fate are harrowing and dispiriting. But Zola always maintained that he was merely portraying things as they were, and even some of his critical opponents conceded the validity of his vision and the need to face the disagreeable facts of slum existence in order to remedy such poverty in the long run. But since environment does have an impact on character, it is not possible to separate them. That indeed is the thrust of Zola's argument. Coupeau, for instance, though already heavily addicted to liquor, undergoes a marked improvement when he spends some time in the country away from the alcoholic fumes and companions of his city district. Whether Gervaise might have behaved differently in another environment and under other circumstances is a provocative question that can never be answered definitively. Zola insists in his preparatory notes that inherited moral qualities do not "overturn free will" ("ne renverse pas le libre arbitre").[30] This contention invites us to examine Gervaise's life so as to see how much choice she does have, and in what ways and to what extent she exercises her free will.

Chapter 6

Gervaise's Choices

Gervaise is the looming central figure in *L'Assommoir*. The story is narrated from her perspective, and often in her voice in free indirect speech; the narrator identifies with her point of view and adopts her language so that the reader gets to know how the character perceives the situation.

Gervaise is one of the recurrent characters in *The Rougon-Macquarts*. The first novel of the series, *The Fortune of the Rougons*, though mainly about Gervaise's mother and her half-brother, Pierre, also includes some details about her early life. Born in 1828, Gervaise is the second illegitimate child of the widowed Adélaïde Rougon and her lover, the good-for-nothing Antoine Macquart. She is bandy-legged from birth, with a slight deformation of her right hip, rather small and underdeveloped in her childhood. As a tonic she is given anisette, a strong alcoholic cordial, but it doesn't do her much good! She has a charming doll's head, round in shape and with delicate features. Her father begrudges her and her sister and brother every piece of clothing, every pair of shoes, every mouthful of food. However, Gervaise turns into a family asset as soon as she can be sent out to work. At age eight she cracks almonds open for a grocer, and then she is apprenticed as a laundress, earning a respectable wage, which finds its way into her father's pocket. Beaten and brought up on the streets with boys, she becomes pregnant at age fourteen by an eighteen-year-old tanner, Lantier. His mother takes the child in and also the next one born four years later; these are Etienne and Claude, who appear in the opening chapter of *L'Assommoir* but who play relatively little part in the novel thereafter. Gervaise's father, though initially indignant is reluctant to press for marriage because it would mean the loss of her wages. It was in fact quite customary at that time among the working class for a young couple to have one or two children before getting married and setting up their own household. Often, as in *Germinal*, the young man would move in with the woman's family, who would have the benefit of his income. Only with the second or third child did the overcrowding necessitate the financial sacrifice of a separate home. To this extent economic factors were implicated in marital habits; Gervaise's case is fairly typical.

When the action of *L'Assommoir* starts, in May 1850, Gervaise has recently moved to Paris with Lantier and the little boys. Lantier has inherited some money, which he has quickly frittered away in the capital so that Gervaise is stranded in a strange city with a broke and unemployed lover, who walks out on her in search of greener pastures. She is then twenty-two years old. She dies in 1869, already an old, worn woman at the age of forty-one. The hardships of women's lives at that time, especially among the poor but at other social levels too—the multiple pregnancies, scant and misguided medical care, inadequate nutrition—all combined to induce rapid aging. There are many references in the course of *L'Assommoir* to the large amount of weight that Gervaise gains, and as she grows stouter she also becomes more ungainly because her weight exacerbates her limp. At the outset, she is an attractive young woman; her physical deterioration is part of her total decline during the nineteen years of the novel's time span.

Zola wants Gervaise to be "an appealing personality" ("un personnage sympathique").[31] As an experienced novelist, he realizes that his pivotal figure must arouse the reader's sympathy. Yet Gervaise lacks any conventional glamor: Zola conceives her as "a beast of burden at work" (1544, "une bête de somme au travail"), with a tender and passionate temperament. She is by no means a simple character, which may be one more reason why Zola decided to change the original title. Every one of her good qualities ironically turns against her: hard work brutalizes her, and her tender-heartedness leads her to extraordinary weaknesses. The sweetness and submissiveness that were the most highly prized traits in a nineteenth-century woman become a source of Gervaise's troubles. The entire working-class world, Zola notes (1544), consciously or unconsciously conspires to destroy her. Again, here is the cardinal role of environment in shaping a character's destiny through the interaction of the outer and the inner worlds.

It is by no means simple to trace exactly what happens to Gervaise in the course of *L'Assommoir*. At first she appears robust, of reasonably good cheer considering her predicament, and possessing all the sound instincts of a survivor. She does her best to clean and tidy the dismal room where she lives at the "Hotel Boncoeur," a pretentiously misnamed flophouse grotesquely lacking in the "Goodheart" proclaimed in its appellation. She withstands the initial setback of being abandoned by Lantier with fortitude after a bout of justified anxiety about her future and that of her children. Her marriage to Coupeau seems to assure her of a modicum of security. She herself emerges as hard-working, competent, resourceful, thrifty, and decent. Her fortune seems to be ascendant, and she is on the verge of success and happiness when she finds the store for her laundry business. But then in the second half of the novel everything sours and collapses. What is it that happens to Gervaise? How does she come to grief despite her positive qualities? What forces coalesce to effect her downfall? Does she make bad choices or is her fate inevitable given the circumstances?

Gervaise is certainly not an overreacher. During the courtship in one of her rare moments of self-reflection, she outlines to Coupeau her aims in life:

> "I'm not at all ambitions, you know, I don't ask for very much. . . .
> My ideal would be to get on quietly with my work, always have

something to eat, have a decent sort of corner to sleep in—you know, just a bed, a table and a couple of chairs, that's all. . . . Oh, and I'd like to bring up my kids and make them into ordinary honest folk if I could. And there's one other thing—not to be beaten if I took up with anybody again; no, I shouldn't fancy being beaten. . . . That's all, really, that's all."

She turned it over in her mind and tried to find out if she wanted anything else, but could not find anything important. Yet she did go on, after some hesitation:

"Yes, I suppose you could wish to end up by dying in your own bed. . . . After toiling and moiling all my life I should be glad to die at home in my own bed." (56; 410–11)

Her ideal is a modest one of domestic contentment with a few luxuries, such as the clock she cherishes, and perhaps the possibility of spending her later days in the peace of the countryside. The absence of some negatives, like being beaten, figures as largely in her projections as the presence of desired elements.

This passage, where Gervaise defines her goals, is a key one in the structure of the novel. Twice further on in the action there are clear echoes of it as she reassesses her current situation against the yardstick she has earlier created. At the height of her success, as her business is about to open, she muses:

After all, hadn't all her dreams come true, and was there anything left for her to wish for in life? She recalled her old ideal when she was down and out: work, food, somewhere to live and bring up her kids, not to be beaten and to die in her own bed. And now that ideal had been more than realized, for she had everything of the very best. And as to dying in her own bed, she added with a laugh, she was counting on that all right, but as late as possible, of course! (145; 402)

Significantly, Gervaise disclaims any credit for being good (145; 502). In other words, she doesn't think in terms of a cause-and-effect relationship between her actions and what happens to her; much rather she attributes success, and later misfortune, to chance in a world ruled by contingencies over which she has no control. Her outlook is one of good-humored but largely passive acceptance of her fate. So she can concede the failure of all her aspirations with a terrible burst of laughter:

> As she climbed the six flights of stairs in the darkness she couldn't stop laughing—a horrible cackle that hurt. She was recalling her old, old ideal: to work steadily, always have something to eat, have a decent place to live in and bring up her children, not be beaten and die in her bed. No, really, it was a scream the way it all worked out! She had no more work, no food left, she slept on filth, her daughter was on the streets, her husband gave her thrashings and all she had left was to peg out in the road, and that would be pretty quick too, if she had the guts to throw herself out of the window as soon as she got up there. Anyone would have thought she had prayed to have thirty thousand a year and be kowtowed to! No, it's perfectly true that in life you may well be modest in your desires and still not have a penny to bless yourself with. Not even food and a bed, that was the common lot. What made her horrible laugh even more bitter was the recollection of her beautiful vision of retirement to the country after twenty years of laundering. Oh well, she was on her way there! She was ready for her plot of grass in Père-Lachaise. (405; 778–79).

The repeated return to the first statement of her aims is used as a choral refrain in *L'Assommoir*, an imaginative means to measure Gervaise's standing and to chart her rise and fall.

One way to read Gervaise's life is as an experiment in determinism. This is the interpretation that Zola proposes when he claims in his preface that "my characters are not bad, but only ignorant and spoilt by the environment of grinding toil and poverty in which they live" (21; 373). The environment has a particularly negative impact on Gervaise because she is not hardened to it, having grown up in the less harsh atmosphere of a small country town. It is also exceptionally treacherous to her insofar as it stimulates the tendency to drink that she has inherited from her father. It is important to remember her strong opposition to drinking at the outset; it is not a temptation, much less a problem to her at the time of her marriage to Coupeau. Yet the physical and moral disposition to alcoholism is latent in her;

she bears its imprint in her limp. As she is absorbed into an environment where alcohol abuse is the norm, as she is repeatedly offered drink, as her husband becomes a burden, her business a failure, her debts overwhelming, and her hopes for the future extinguished: in these circumstances her hereditary weakness reasserts itself, and she yields to the consolation of liquor in compliance with the custom of her surroundings.

Her environment is made up of three overlapping elements: the district, the housing, and the people who live there. Gervaise is directly affected by all of them. The district is a grim working-class area, whose inhabitants are huddled into hideous slums. The threatening aspects of such an environment are immediately brought out in the opening chapter as Gervaise sits at the window watching the men stream to work:

> The herd went on trampling past the barrier in the chilly morning. You could tell the locksmiths by their blue overalls, masons by their white jackets, painters by their coats with long smocks showing underneath. From a distance this crowd looked a uniformly nondescript plaster colour, a neutral tone made up chiefly of faded blue and dirty grey. Now and again some workman would stop to light his pipe, but the others tramped on round him with never a smile, never a word to a mate, pasty faces all turned towards Paris, which swallowed them one by one down the gaping hole of the Faubourg Poissonnière. All the same, some of them did slacken their pace at the two corners of the rue des Poissonniers in front of two bars where the shutters were being taken down, but before going in they hesitated on the pavement, casting sidelong glances Pariswards, arms dangling loose, already won over to a day off work. At the counters groups were already standing each other rounds of drinks, hanging about, filling up the bars, spitting, coughing, giving their throats a rinse with tots of spirits. (25–26; 378)

The city is here personified as a monster with gaping jaws lurking to devour people, like the mine in *Germinal*. This is a powerful image of fear that is impressed on Gervaise's mind (and on the reader's) at the very outset. The menace is reiterated in the unfriendliness of the workers toward each other, the lack of solidarity, each one enclosed in his own worries without heed of neighbors. The group is dehumanized and reduced to the level of animals in the word "herd" ("troupeau"). The sinister lure of liquor is also shown as some of the men slink off into bars instead of going to work. In this one paragraph, with utmost economy, Zola has introduced several of the major features of this environment: its active hostility, its fostering of self-centeredness, and its encouragement to drink.

The focal point of the district is Old Colombe's bar, to which even most of the good workers gravitate near the end of the day. It seems to cast a kind of spell that puzzles Gervaise when she is first taken there by Coupeau during their courtship. It is through Gervaise's eyes that the reader sees the bar:

> By now the pub was full. Everybody was talking at the top of his voice, with isolated shoutings cutting through the general hubbub of hoarse voices. Fists banging on the counter set glasses jingling. The drinkers were all standing about in little knots, with hands crossed over their stomachs or behind their backs, so tightly were they crammed together, and there were groups at the back near the casks who had a quarter of an hour's wait before they could order their round from Old Colombe.
>
> "Well, if it isn't our posh Cadet-Cassis!" bawled Mes-Bottes, slapping Coupeau hard across the shoulders. "A gent what smokes cigarettes and sports a clean shirt! Wants to impress his lady friend, I suppose, and is pushing the boat out!"
>
> "Leave me alone, see!" answered Coupeau, very put out.
>
> The other just grinned.
>
> "O. K. Very 'oity-toity, aren't we? Well, I say a shit's always a shit, so there!"
>
> He gave Gervaise a dirty leer and turned his back. She shrank away, rather frightened. The pipe smoke and the strong smell of all these men, mingled with the fumes of alcohol, caught her breath and made her cough. (55; 409–10)

The mainspring and, in a literal sense, the source of this drinking subculture is the bizarre distilling machine housed in a little yard behind the bar under a clear glass roof. Gervaise is curious to see it, but she immediately recognizes it as "dour and forbidding" (57; 511) and exclaims: "that machine gives me the creeps" (57; 512). She recoils instinctively from the fountainhead of the district's depravity.

Gervaise's housing marks the stages of her rise and fall, acting as a barometer of her economic standing. In the miserable room at the Hotel Boncoeur of the first chapter she is at a fairly low point, but hopeful of improvement as she cleans and tidies. After her marriage to Coupeau she moves into a small, pleasant apartment near her place of employment:

> At last they had a find, a big room with a little room opening out of it and a kitchen, in the rue Neuve de la Goutte d'Or, almost opposite the laundry. It was in a little two-storey house with a very steep flight of stairs leading up to only two flats, one to the right and the other to the left, the ground floor being the living quarters of a man who hired out carriages which were stabled all round a big yard opening on to the road. Gervaise was delighted, and thought she was back in the country; no neighbours, no gossiping to worry about, a peaceful corner that reminded her of a quiet lane in Plassans behind the ramparts and, as the final stroke of luck, she could keep an eye on her own window from her ironing-board, without even putting her iron down, by just stretching her neck. (108; 464)

The relative tranquility of this small building in a street with the promising name "New Drop of Gold" is reminiscent of Gervaise's early more rural surroundings. Compared to the large and noisy tenement house, where the Coupeaus had originally thought of living, this is a sheltered haven. In the Goujets they have fine neighbors who serve as positive role models. Gervaise is ingenious in fixing and furnishing the room, dividing it with white calico curtains; with its fireplace, two rows of family photos, and a chest (her pride and joy), it has the air of a cozy home. The chest in particular, because it is so solid, is a symbol of the respectability that she has attained. Gervaise spends four years in this little apartment, working twelve hours a day in the

laundry across the road. During this time Nana is born. The Coupeaus
are well regarded "as a steady couple who kept themselves to themselves," who maintained their home "as bright as a new pin" (107;
463), who had decent earnings, didn't drink too much, took Sunday
walks, and saved quite a bit. For this short period the calm environment of this quiet preserve of the city, together with the good example
set by the neighbors, has a positive effect on Gervaise.

The move into the big house initiates a new phase in Gervaise's
life. Ever since her first visit there, before her marriage, to see Coupeau's sister, she has been simultaneously attracted and repelled by this
place:

> Gervaise looked up at the front of the building. On the street side
> it had five floors, each one with fifteen windows in a line, the black
> shutters of which, with their broken slats, gave the huge wall-space
> a look of utter desolation. But below that there were four shops on
> the ground floor: to the right of the doorway a huge sleazy eating-
> house, to the left a coal merchant's, a draper's and an umbrella
> shop. The building looked all the more colossal because it stood
> between two low rickety houses clinging to either side of it and,
> foursquare, like a roughly cast block of cement, decaying and flak-
> ing away in the rain, it thrust the silhouette of its vast cube up into
> the pale sky above the neighbouring rooftops. Its unplastered sides,
> mud-coloured and as interminably bare as prison walls, showed
> rows of toothing-stones like decaying jaws snapping in the void. But
> Gervaise's attention was mainly caught by the doorway, an immense
> arched entrance going up to the second floor level and opening like
> a deep porch, at the further end of which could be seen the dim
> light of a large courtyard. In the middle of this porch, which was
> paved like the street, ran a gulley along which some pale pink water
> was flowing.
> "Come on in," said Coupeau, "nobody's going to eat you." (59;
> 413–14)

Although the narration here is in the third-person, the house is actually perceived through Gervaise's eyes; the repeated use of "look"
and "looked" underscores that it is her impression. She is fascinated

71

by its gigantic size, probably far greater than anything she had ever seen in Plassans, and as she enters the courtyard and looks round again, she is also struck by its teeming life. The house is a microcosmic replica of the city. Gervaise's desire to live there may express her subconscious wish to become part of Paris. On the other hand, the nasty and frightening aspects of the house are inescapable. A large proportion of the words used in this description have a distinctly negative charge: "black," "broken," "utter desolation," "sleazy," "rickety," "decaying and flaking away in the rain," "mud-coloured and as interminably bare as prison walls," "toothing-stones like decaying jaws snapping in the void." The motif of jaws links the house to Gervaise's earlier vision of the city as a monster prepared to swallow up the workmen. Coupeau's intended reassurance to her, "nobody's going to eat you" has an ironic ring, especially in retrospect, since the house does in a sense eat Gervaise up. But at this first encounter her attention fixes mainly on the more welcoming features: the light beckoning into the courtyard and the pale pink effluent from the dye-works with its promise of prettiness. She dwells on the engaging possibilities, too, when she chooses what could be "her own window, a window in the left-hand corner where there was a little window-box with some scarlet runners in it, the delicate tendrils of which were beginning to wind in and out of a network of string" (59; 416). Again, a context for irony is here created: instead of living in a room with a blooming window box, Gervaise will die in a windowless and unventilated hole.

At first, however, in her new business Gervaise prospers both financially and personally. Her shop opens out onto the street, and she enjoys standing in the doorway "to beam at the street at large, bursting with the shopkeeper's pride in her own little bit of pavement" (143; 500). The situation is somewhat reminiscent of that in the opening chapter with Gervaise looking out of the window. The parallel serves to emphasize the difference: now Gervaise is married, established in her enterprise; she is also on street level and hence integrated into the district. As in the previous scene, she looks to the right and then to the left, but what she sees now is pleasing and exciting: "Gervaise loved the street" (143; 500). She in turn is well liked and respected by her neighbors. She appears expansively in this scene almost to take possession of the street and the area, and certainly to feel at home there. The house gives her a definite base, and nurtures the hope that she will indeed be able to achieve her aims. The water from the dye-works, a symbolic indicator of her mood, is in the most delicate colors while her relationship to her environment is so favorable. What remains unchanged is the point of view, focalized through Gervaise's eyes as she stands and looks.

Even after Coupeau's accident and the onset of her financial troubles, Gervaise maintains an open interchange with the street. On cold winter afternoons the "shop was a haven of refuge for all the chilly people in the neighborhood, for the whole of the rue de la Goutte d'Or knew it was nice and warm there" (191; 552). Gervaise befriends poor people shivering outside, and invites them to share her heating. In reaching out in this way, she builds a bridge between herself and her environment; she improves the area for others, but, characteristically, runs the risk of harm to herself through her generosity. This behavior pattern is apparent again at her birthday party. The good smell of the goose spreads over the house and the street as a healthy counteragent to the usual alcoholic and other evil odors. Gervaise, extending her hospitality to the destitute, invites Old Bru to partake of the feast. Eventually the whole district looks in through the open door and joins in the celebration. Gervaise is at the climax of her success, queen of the neighborhood. Whereas before she was looking out at them, now they are looking in to her; the outsider has become the insider.

This position is reversed with her decline, and she reverts again to being a lone figure looking out from her window onto the courtyard. Her quarters are now so restricted (and she has become so large) that only by wedging herself between the wall and the chest and giving herself a stiff neck can she see out at all. Her enclosure is symbolically rendered in this scene, and so is the withering of her hopes as she gazes out and realizes how far she has fallen short of her early aspirations.

But the courtyard almost always gave her the miseries. There opposite she could see her dream of long ago, that fifth-floor window

where every springtime the runner beans coiled their delicate tendrils round a network of strings. Her own room was on the shady
side, and pots of mignonette were dead within a week. Oh no, life
wasn't turning out all that good, it wasn't at all the existence she
had hoped for. Instead of having flowers round her in her old age
she was drifting towards things that were not at all nice. One day,
as she leaned down she had such a funny sensation. She thought
she saw herself down there under the archway, by the concierge's
lodge, staring up and examining the building for the first time, and
this jump back of thirteen years made her heart miss a beat. The
yard looked just the same, the bare walls were hardly more black
and flaking than they were then; the same stench was coming up
from the rusty drainpipes, washing was still hanging on lines across
the windows, with babies' nappies caked with filth as of old. At the
bottom the uneven paving was still messy with the locksmith's cin-
ders and the carpenter's shavings, and in the wet corner by the tap
there was even a puddle from the dyeworks of the same pale blue
as years ago. But she herself, she felt, was pretty different and shop-
soiled. She was no longer down there looking up skywards, happy
and brave, planning a nice home. She was in a garret in the lousy
part, in the dingiest hole where no friendly ray of sunshine ever
came. (306–7; 672–73)

Gervaise's perception of her environment acts as a yardstick to her
situation, and she uses her response to the house to take stock of herself in an echo of her initial statement of her life aims. As the city is
progressively rebuilt and gentrified, it offers a stark contrast to the
ruination for which she is heading. Her annoyance and alienation express in part her disappointment with herself for her failure. The house
acts as both an ideal and an abomination in Gervaise's mind, giving it
a bipolar effect. She tries to attain its best, symbolized by a sunny
window with a flower box on which she sets her desires, but she is
dragged down into the mire of its depravity that swallows up any
goodness. Gervaise's relationship to her environment proves consid-
erably more complex than the experiment in determinism that Zola
envisaged.

At the end Gervaise believes in the house's essential malevolence
and wonders why it took her so long to recognize this. "To think that

so long ago she had aspired to live in a corner of this great bare barrack. Her ears must have been stopped that she couldn't hear the awful hymn of despair being sung behind those walls! From the very first day that she had set foot in the place she had been going downhill. It must bring ill-luck to be piled one on top of another in these miserable great working-class tenements in which penury was infectious, like the cholera" (405; 778).

The image of disease here is important because it reveals Gervaise's own consciousness of the negative impact on her of her environment. What is more, the spread of an infectious disease is beyond the control of willpower, as it hits the virtuous and the corrupt alike, with an indifference to morality. It could be argued that Gervaise is merely making excuses for herself by seeing the house as the source of evil. Zola does not actually let her transfer blame for all of her misfortune onto the environment. She records the growth of her bad luck only "from the day that she had set foot in" the house; strictly speaking even this is not accurate, for she does prosper for a while. However, on a deeper human and poetic level Gervaise's lament is true insofar as the dominant atmosphere in the house and in the district militates against decency.

It is in this context that Gervaise's human environment assumes its main significance. She is encircled by people who show signs of demoralization in one way or another. The scene is quickly set in the opening chapter with the seriocomic battle with Virginie in the washing establishment, which vividly evokes the coarse strife rampant in this milieu. Lantier's willful desertion of Gervaise and of their children is another immediate pointer to the prevailing ethic of self-interest. He manages to lead a calculatedly parasitic existence, devouring one household after another without ever doing a stroke of work and apparently without coming to any harm. On the contrary, he does remarkably well for himself by means of his self-serving posturing. His capacity to thrive suggests the inverse relationship in this world between honesty and success. Lantier is perhaps the most vicious and sinister figure in *L'Assommoir* because he is impelled by cold scheming for his own advantage. Coupeau and his drinking companions are bad role models too, but their debasement is, at least in part, the outcome of despair. In liquor they find a short-term escape from the problems in their lives. Though they are a jovial group, the possible grim consequences of alcohol abuse are illustrated in the murderous Bijart. Gervaise is a witness to the ill-treatment suffered by Lalie without being able to do anything to help her. Lalie, together with Goujet, represent the good, who are far outnumbered here by the bad and by the indifferent, who go with the wind. Gervaise's own impulsive kindness is an incongruous quality in this environment.

Given her heredity, her environment, and her situation, what then are Gervaise's prospects? Many readers maintain that she has little or no chance of making a reasonable life for herself, and deplore the brooding fatalism that hangs over *L'Assommoir*. That, of course, is a consequence of Zola's experiment in determinism, which loads the dice against his protagonists. But there is evidence that Gervaise does herself contribute to her downfall through her character and her actions. It is this that gives the novel its tragic edge and makes it a masterpiece of world literature rather than an exposition of nineteenth-century thought.

Gervaise's choices, admittedly, are severely limited by her station in the class hierarchy, by her financial exigency, and not least by her gender. Whereas a young man of the period was free to go out and seek his fortune, as so many novels record, a young woman was much more bound by social conventions. Marriage was the normal expectation, indeed the only conceivable path at every level of society. That Gervaise has fallen in with Lantier and had two children by him while still in her teens is not unusual for her class and time. How much conscious choice she has exercised in following him to Paris is hard to decide. Not much, probably, since she would have been ostracized by her family in Plassans if she had stayed behind, and, more important, once she has his two children, she is financially dependent on Lantier. Women's wages were so low that a single woman could not support her children and herself without the grossest hardship. Gervaise's legal position vis-a-vis Lantier is ambiguous. On marriage a woman and her property became her husband's possession, literally a chattel, deprived of the right to existence as an independent entity under the law. As a common-law wife, without the protection of the marital contract, Gervaise's situation would be even more exiguous since Lantier would be under no obligation to support her. It is likely that Gervaise went to Paris on the assumption that he would soon marry her, although she confides to Madame Boche in the washing establishment that he is not so nice that one would want to be his wife. While capable of momentary rebellion against Lantier's demands, by and large Gervaise acquiesces in submission, and accepts her lot as typical: "It happened like it always does" (35; 388). She has surprisingly few illusions about him, recognizing that he "has grand ideas and goes through his money" (36; 389).

When Lantier suddenly ditches her without any warning, Gervaise is left in a desperate plight: in a city where she knows no one, without adequate means of support, with two small children, and with all her belongings already pawned. The drama of this abrupt drop in her fortunes comes across in the little boys' innocent, loud announcement in the washing establishment: "Daddy's gone" (40; 393). The impact of the alliterative French phrase is greater: "Papa est parti." Trying to avoid the gravity of this news, Gervaise at first misunderstands and interprets it to mean that Lantier has gone out to fetch dinner. Only when she learns that he has taken all his things away in his trunk in a cab does she grasp the crisis facing her. Her stunned silence, her tears, and her somber reflections at the close of the first chapter indicate her understanding of her predicament as well as her sense of powerlessness to remedy it.

Three weeks later, at the beginning of chapter 2, Gervaise is having a brandy at Old Colombe's bar with Coupeau. He has been casually mentioned in the opening chapter as a roofer then living on the top floor at the Hotel Boncoeur. In contrast to Lantier, Coupeau has a positive aura. He is described as "friendly-like," as he addresses Gervaise in "a bright young voice" (35; 377). His obvious interest in her after Lantier's disappearance would seem to be a godsend to her, for he is an attractive match, a good worker with a pleasant personality. Considering her dire situation, one would expect Gervaise to jump at this opportunity, especially as Coupeau talks of marriage right away. The choice between destitution and marriage to Coupeau is, in Gervaise's circumstances—with two dependent children—a non-choice. She must marry him, and it isn't a disagreeable forced alliance since he is genuinely fond of her and treats her with affection and respect.

Yet Gervaise hangs back. Her hesitancy at this point is one of the puzzles of *L'Assommoir*. There can be no doubt that she is sufficiently realistic to appraise her future with or without Coupeau and to seize this great chance. She isn't playing "hard-to-get," as a young nubile middle- or upper-class woman with a dowry might, not accepting a first offer of marriage out of coyness. Gervaise gives Coupeau two cogent reasons for her demur, but they amount to twin aspects of the same fact: that she has two children. She doesn't want to burden him with another man's offspring, and she feels ashamed for him in front of the neighbors, who have seen her with her lover. Gervaise clearly has certain culturally conditioned inhibitions, including a code of morality that sanctions her cohabitation with Lantier but does not extend to bringing this "funny dowry" to Coupeau and "cluttering him up with two kids" (64; 419). She may fear that as stepchildren Etienne and Claude would be second-class citizens in the family. What is more likely is that she remains attached to Lantier despite his abominable behavior. Madame Boche in the washing establishment realizes this, and when she says, "You're still in love with him, aren't you, poor dear?" (41; 394), Gervaise does not deny it. This continuing deep devotion to Lantier is important to note at this early point because of its later role in the motivation of the action. It is the expression of one of Zola's cherished notions, which he explored in his early novel *Madeleine Férat* (1868), that a woman is somehow emotionally and physically tied for life to her first love.

It is Gervaise's heart and her body, rather than her reckoning intelligence, that make her give in to Coupeau's pleas. The element of sensuality is sharply underscored here on both sides. Coupeau dismisses Gervaise's objections with the blunt statement that "he wanted her" (65; 420). She in turn is affected by "this atmosphere of animal desire which she felt all around her" (65; 420) in old Colombe's bar. This is an instance where environment plays an unmistakable part in determining action. But it is also a passage that gave offense at the time because sexual urges in women were not admitted. The moment of consent is portrayed with great psychological delicacy:

> Seeing her at a loss for arguments, silently and vaguely smiling, Coupeau seized her hand and pulled her towards him. She was in one of those unguarded moods she was so afraid of, when she was quite won over and too deeply moved to refuse anything or hurt anybody's feelings. But he did not realize that she was giving herself to him, and all he did was go on squeezing her wrists so hard that he made them hurt, and in this way took possession of her. Each breathed a long sigh at this slight pain in which each found a partial satisfaction of their longing.
>
> "You do say yes, don't you?"
>
> "Oh, you really are a nuisance," she murmured. "So you really mean it? All right then, yes. Oh dear, but we're doing something very silly, perhaps." (65; 420)

Although Gervaise makes a wise decision, taking the only judicious alternative open to her, she in fact does so for rather bad reasons: submissiveness, fear of hurting others' feelings, a need for compliance. These are the qualities to which nineteenth-century women were socialized as desirable, indeed essential, to their role in life as wives and mothers. Gervaise has these qualities to a fault. While it makes no difference in this case, since she has so little choice, in future turning points her soft-heartedness leads to trouble.

That is undoubtedly what happens after Coupeau's accident, when Gervaise does have genuine alternatives. In contrast to her marked slowness in opting for marriage, she makes up her mind instantaneously and authoritatively to nurse him at home, notwithstanding the expense. The marriage has proved happy; after several years Gervaise is deeply concerned for her husband's welfare. She is prepared, without a moment's thought, to disburse her long accumulated savings, even if it means sacrificing her dream of an independent business. Gervaise shows an innate nobility and a touching loyalty to her husband in this instinctive response. Ironically, *L'Assommoir* suggests, such altruism does not pay in this environment.

Gervaise also makes a choice in accepting a loan from Goujet to finance her business. She does so after only scant protest. She does not, however, initiate this transaction, nor does she enter into any formal agreement about it. For a married woman this would have been impossible because she did not exist as an independent legal entity. Gervaise takes the loan in the firm belief that she will be able to make regular repayments, as she does for a while, but her problems eventually overwhelm her so that she defaults on this debt.

How much choice Gervaise has in her handling of Coupeau during his convalescence is a moot question. Theoretically, she could gradually ease him back to work by encouraging and supporting him, and ultimately push him to resume his obligations as head of the household. But such tough love is not at all Gervaise's style. She infantilizes and coddles him, largely because she so enjoys being kind to people and making their lives pleasant. She is not sufficiently astute to realize the effect of such pandering on Coupeau. While adopting her point of view and her voice, the narrator makes plain her responsibility for the turn of events:

> She no longer had the bother of lifting off and putting back the glass dome of the clock, for all the savings had gone and she had to work, and work hard, work for four, because there were four mouths to feed and she was the only one to feed the lot of them. Yet when she heard people sympathizing with her she hastened to excuse Coupeau. But just think what he had gone through! It wasn't surprising if he had gone a bit grumpy. But it wouldn't last after he had got well again. And if it was hinted that Coupeau seemed quite fit now and could perfectly well go back to work, she protested; no, no, not yet! She didn't want to have him back in bed again. She knew what the doctor had told her, didn't she? She was the one who prevented him from going to work by repeating every morning that he must take his time and not force the pace. She even slipped the odd franc piece now and again into his waistcoat pocket. Coupeau accepted this as quite natural, and he complained of all sorts of ills so as to

be coddled; six months later his convalescence was still going on. (133; 489–90)

But even if Gervaise must be given part of the blame, this does not necessarily mean that she has freedom of choice. She acts according to the dictates of her character, which is a product of her genes and her upbringing, and her conditioning as a woman whose primary duty is to be agreeable to her husband. Another woman, however, Madame Goujet, notices early on how Coupeau is turning bad, too indolent to use the time of his convalescence to learn to read. Gervaise evades the emergence of his nasty tendencies for many reasons: she is too close to the situation and too beholden to him as his wife; she is too preoccupied with keeping the household going and getting her business established; and finally, but really above all, she doesn't want to confront unpleasantness. Perhaps this is her way of dealing with an environment that is full of distress.

When Coupeau at long last goes back to work, Gervaise gives him money for his lunch, a drink, and a smoke. But on two days out of six he stops for a drink on his way to work and never gets there, like some of the workmen Gervaise had seen in her dawn watch at the window in the first chapter. The details of that opening scene are carefully designed to foreshadow events in the novel, taking on retrospective meaning as we read further. Coupeau drifts home with all sorts of excuses by lunchtime, and hangs out idly in Gervaise's laundry. The stench of the dirty linen, especially in summer, induces a kind of dazed stupor: "her first bouts of laziness dated from this moment, in the asphyxiating fumes of these old clothes spreading their poisonous miasma around her" (149; 506). In this atmosphere she yields to Coupeau's amorous advances: "But he had hold of her and wouldn't let her go. She abandoned herself, feeling a bit giddy with this mountain of washing and not in the least upset by Coupeau's boozy breath. And the smacking kiss they gave each other full on the mouth amidst the filth of her trade was a sort of first step downwards in their slow descent into squalor" (152; 509). This episode, as the narrator points out, is a major landmark in their decline. The French term "avachissement" is much more colorful than the English translation "slow descent into squalor"; its root, *vache* (cow), suggests an atavistic reversion to animalistic behavior, a regression that represents the accompanying countercurrent to the Darwinian theory of evolution.

Gervaise's decline has therefore begun well before it becomes apparent to others. Her stupendous birthday feast, at the center of the novel in chapter 7, marks the climax of her prestige as she seduces the district to celebrate with her. It is a brilliantly articulated extravaganza that reaches its high point in Gervaise's triumphant entry bearing the goose. Its coarseness, which was regarded as scabrous when *L'Assommoir* appeared, is a form of humor, an interlude of joviality in an often gloom-ridden story. As a set piece, it seems to expand digressively, halting the advance of the action. But one of the novel's crucial happenings occurs under cover of the festivity: Lantier's return into Gervaise's life.

That she should consent to this is extremely perplexing. Lantier has treated her so badly and unjustly that she must harbor considerable resentment against him even if its edge has worn off over the years. Her relationship to Coupeau has deteriorated significantly as a result of his drinking, but on the surface the marriage is still intact, sustained by lust and a certain crude affection on both sides. It seems inconceivable that Gervaise should be willing to tolerate the presence of her former lover, not to speak of the additional housekeeping and financial burden of another man to tend. Admittedly, Lantier moves back in as a boarder who will more than pay his way and buttress the family's crumbling budget. However, he soon reneges on this so that even as an economic proposition his presence is not a good development. The total absence of protest on Gervaise's part at this juncture is astonishing.

Her posture becomes comprehensible only through close analysis of the circumstances. Before his appearance, during the preparations for the party, Gervaise hears rumors of Lantier's having been sighted in the district. Although she tries to dismiss this news, it deeply disturbs her. There is a distinct impression that she has learned to fear him, apprehensive both of the havoc he has wrought in her life and of the power he may still wield over her. Earlier, through her renewed friendship with Virginie, she has come to feel "haunted" by the idea of Lantier, admitting to herself that "it came over her in spite of herself" (183; 543). The thought of him gives her a burning sensation in her stomach, but their children form an unbreakable link between them. When he reappears, it is evident from the first mention of his name that she is as curious about him as she is frightened, possibly still as much attracted as repelled. As the first man in her life, her companion for eight years, and the father of her two children, he still has a hold on her, or so Zola believed. Her reaction to him is almost a Pavlovian conditioned reflex. With her usual habit of avoiding difficult issues or hardheaded ratiocination, she busies herself instead with arrangements for the dinner in the hope that the problem will go away.

It is Coupeau who extends the actual invitation to Lantier, in the confusion of the intoxicated revelry when it passes virtually unnoticed. Gervaise would not want to take a stand, even if that were her nature, and risk a scene in front of her guests. Coupeau has been difficult enough already; the start of the dinner had to be delayed and a search made of the local bars to find him. By the time he is brought back he is quite merry, and with all the additional liquor at the feast, he could turn rough. As always, Gervaise is intent on steering clear of any immediate vexation:

> Gervaise stared from one to the other stupidly. At first, when her husband had pushed her old lover into the shop, she had taken her head between her hands with the same instinctive movement that she did in thunderstorms at every clap. It didn't seem possible; the walls must surely fall down and crush everybody. But later, seeing the two men sitting there, and not even the muslin curtains stirring, it suddenly all seemed quite natural. Of course the goose had not agreed with her, and she had certainly had too much of it, which prevented her thinking clearly. She was enveloped in a blissful, numbing laziness which kept her sitting huddled at the table with only one wish, not to be bothered. What the hell was the use of getting all worked up when nobody else was, and things seemed to

be working out on their own to everyone's satisfaction? So she got
up and went to see if there was any coffee left. (229–30; 592)

She lets things slide partly out of physical laziness caused by overeating, but largely because she has "only one wish, not to be bothered."
Her accommodating temperament dictates her silence; never firm or
resistant, she is most yielding toward the end of the party, when she
has herself not only eaten hugely but also drunk a fair amount. Her
mental fuzziness encourages her optimistic assumption, which is really
the expression of a wish, that things will sort themselves out on their
own without thought or effort on her part, and particularly without
any uncomfortable confrontation. The reflexive verb in French, *s'ar-
ranger*, strongly suggests a passive attitude in which events are allowed
to take their course instead of being directed. Gervaise adopts the position traditional to women in the nineteenth century by not raising
her voice and concentrating instead on a homemaking task: she goes
off to see to more coffee. She manages quickly to put Lantier into a
far corner of her mind.

Through her incapacity to face the problem squarely, to speak
out, let alone to assert herself, Gervaise commits an error of omission
for which she pays dearly. The following Saturday, when Coupeau
brings Lantier home to dinner, Gervaise recalls that on the day of her
birthday she "had only seen him through a mist" (234; 597). Even
now, in a sober state, she mutters, "oh yes, of course . . . of course" in
a posture of submission "with downcast eyes, not quite knowing what
she was saying" (234; 597). She lets things happen to her, mutely
acceding to Lantier's assurance that she is now like a sister to him.
Gervaise behaves as if in a daze, and is completely outwitted by Lantier, who is aided and abetted by Coupeau. The latter's motivation in
bringing Lantier into the household is not at all clear. Perhaps his
drinking has deprived him of the ability to think coherently, or he may
want a buffer between himself and Gervaise, who is patently dis-
pleased by his recent conduct. Only Lantier is consciously calculating
his advantage: he brings bunches of violets for Gervaise and her two
assistants, bestows a fatherly kiss on Etienne, and generally goes out

of his way to make a good impression. So much so that he soon charms the household and the whole neighborhood as "a distinguished gentleman" (236; 599) whose visits are an honor. Zola shows here how well Lantier succeeds in bamboozling everyone, including the implacable Lorilleux, and gradually insinuates himself into their good graces through flattery and a deliberate campaign to ingratiate himself.

In the face of this growing public opinion in Lantier's favor Gervaise is even less in a position to hold out against him. She has the same sensations in her stomach as when she thought of him earlier, compounded by attacks of panic and dread lest he should take it into his head to kiss her one night when he finds her alone. Her subconscious is sending her danger signals and anticipating the future course of events. The intensity of her fears is a measure of his grasp on her. But again she backs away from facing the issue; she allows herself to be reassured by Virginie, who makes her feel ashamed of her distrust of Lantier. Over the months he becomes so close a friend of Coupeau's and so frequent a visitor in the household that it is merely a small step to have him live there. This move is therefore the culmination of a long process: on his part as well-designed scheme to worm his way into a cozy nook, and on Gervaise's part a timorous, irresolute drifting. She does not understand the implications, financial or moral, of having Lantier in her home. She responds emotionally and psychosomatically in her stomach; however, she is not capable of thinking things through in concrete terms. As a woman she has been conditioned to acquiesce, not to query. By conforming to this norm by silently going along with her husband's initiatives, Gervaise abdicates choice. She achieves short-term harmony at the cost of long-term disruption.

The pressures that Gervaise feels from then on are vividly expressed in the dream she has one night: that she is poised on the edge of a pit, with Coupeau pushing her with a punch and Lantier tickling her behind to make her jump sooner. This nightmare reveals her awareness of being trapped in a horrible position, into which she is being further impelled by the impact of the two men. In this situation she is clearly the helpless victim. The dream does not tell her, nor does she know, how she came to this impasse. She envisages herself as devoid of choice, as indeed she increasingly has been. But somewhere, probably as early as her decision to marry Coupeau, she made the woman's choice of compliance with the wishes of others, and her entire life ever since has been a record of yielding. What, on the other hand, have been her alternatives? Her only viable chance of escape comes in Goujet's offer that they go away together to start a new life in Belgium. Gervaise spontaneously turns him down: "It isn't possible, Monsieur Goujet. It would be very wrong. I'm a married woman, you see, with children . . ." (253; 616–17). Gervaise here shows a noble sense of duty toward her family. Her predominant self-image as "a married woman" determines her responses as well as her silences.

The question of Gervaise's choices arises once more in an acute crisis when she comes home one night with Lantier to find that Coupeau has soiled the bed and the room with his vomit. Her revulsion at the sight marks a breaking point, "a rude blow to any feeling his wife might still have" (266; 631). Her stomach knots, and she recoils from touching him as if his body were the corpse of someone who had died of a foul disease. As in her initial acceptance of Coupeau, so in her final rejection of him, the physical component plays a central role. Coupeau has, literally, made himself untouchable in behavior that Gervaise perceives as not only subhuman, but subanimal.

Her immediate problem is finding a place to sleep. She tries to climb over him, but his vomit bars all access to the bed, not to mention the stench. There is no denying the disgustingness of this scene with all its gross detail; hostile critics often cited it as the acme of bad taste and applied to *L'Assommoir* Lantier's exclamation as he enters the room, "It stinks to high heaven" (266; 630). What the critics overlooked is the dramatic necessity of this ugliness as a motivation for Gervaise's ultimate surrender to Lantier. Under the circumstances it is natural that he should offer her the hospitality of his bed, especially given their earlier relationship. Gervaise resists and struggles vigorously; she is now actually in a situation reminiscent of her nightmare—on the verge of a precipice, with Coupeau's vomit giving her

the push while Lantier's endearments egg her on. Her practical concern with finding a bed conflicts with her moral sense of propriety,
particularly in view of Nana's and Grandma Coupeau's presence in
the adjacent room. She continues to fob Lantier off until he stops urg-
ing her verbally and instead slowly kisses "her ear, just he used to in
the old days, to tease her. The strength went out of her and she was
conscious of a great buzzing in her head and a great shudder running
through her flesh" (268; 632). It is the physical attraction of Lantier
in the memories aroused by his kiss, combined with the physical re-
pulsiveness of Coupeau, that makes Gervaise cede to her old lover.
Again, as in her acceptance of Coupeau's proposal of marriage, Zola
introduces the woman's sensuality as a decisive factor. Gervaise is
shown in the grip of feelings more powerful than her reason; her
choice is made for her by the gut reactions of her body.

The pattern of Gervaise's behavior under the pressure of circumstances makes it evident that she is caught in a vicious circle: her heredity and environment combine with societal expectations of a
woman's conduct to determine her character, which in turn affects her
handling of critical dilemmas. Her central trait is a softness that is
manifest in her attitude to herself as well as to others, with disastrous
results in both instances. Although not generally self-conscious or reflective, Gervaise is aware of this feature of her personality. In her
confessional conversation with Coupeau, when they discuss marriage
and she outlines her aims in life, she admits to this fault: "Her only
weakness, she said, was that she was over-kind, she liked everybody,
she devoted herself to people who only paid her back by hurting her"
(53; 408). Her humane compassion toward those worse off than herself is one of her most attractive characteristics. She shows great generosity to her mother-in-law, taking her in and supporting her when
she can ill afford to do so, whereas the old woman's own daughters
are mean and stingy to their mother. Equally striking is Gervaise's
compassion for Old Bru, a forlorn, destitute, somewhat confused old
man, whom she feeds and shelters on many occasions. Lalie Bijard she
cannot help substantively, but she extends sympathy and understanding to her. Despite all the misery she has already seen in the house,

and despite her own problems, the death of Lalie really tears at Gervaise's heart.

By instinct, therefore, Gervaise is a nurturing mother figure, who wants to care for others and make life better for them. Curiously, however, she is not seen in *L'Assommoir* as devoting much attention to any of her children. Etienne and Claude have no part in the action after the opening chapter; Claude is sent back to the south to be brought up by a gentleman interested in his gift for painting, while Etienne is apprenticed at the bolt and rivet factory and taken under Goujet's wing. As for Nana, she is left to sprout like a weed in the increasing disorder of the household. Gervaise's relationships to her children seem to bear out one of the main objections to women working raised by social thinkers of the time: that their children would suffer neglect. Since Gervaise's work is at home, the problem stems not from her absence but from her inability to meet the excessive demands on her time, attention, and financial resources. And because she is impulsive and spontaneous, she is not judicious in directing her kindness. So she under-cares for her children and at the same time over-cares for Coupeau.

The dangers of Gervaise's softness are connected to her unwillingness to say no. Except for Goujet's offer to start a new life together in Belgium, she never refuses anything; she is described as "amiable to everybody . . . meek as a lamb and as sweet as sugar" (145; 502). She cannot bear to hurt people, she wants life to be nice, and she has a naive and benevolent desire to see others happy. This results in her repeated yielding to the wishes of others, particularly her husband. She is, of course, fulfilling the woman's pledge of obedience and submissiveness, but she does so too well, to her own damage. Her tolerance of Lantier's return is the supreme example of the harm done to her by her forbearance although it is complicated by her fear of Coupeau, who is by then liable to alcohol induced fits of rage. Ironically, her simple wish for universal happiness produces in the end only almost universal misery. Her disposition to comply and to oblige is well encompassed in the French word *complaisance*, which does not have the same meaning as the English "complacency." It denotes rather a mentality that finds its own central gratification in pleasing others. This was unequivocally the ideal held up to women in the nineteenth century. It is part of the tragedy of Gervaise's life that she comes to grief by playing out the role assigned to her to excess. Her sense of self-preservation is swamped by her urge to please.

Gervaise's softness leads to her tendency to accommodate as a way of following the path of least resistance. She deals with unpleasant circumstances not by fighting or trying to amend them, but by adapting to them. This motif is reiterated in *L'Assommoir*; Gervaise gets used to everything: to the mess created by the dirty linen, to Lantier's comings and goings, to foul language and abuse, to the move to more cramped quarters, to Coupeau's increasingly violent sprees, even to juggling her two men side by side:

> She would have liked to change skins when she changed men. But gradually she got used to it. It's too tiring to have to have a bath every time! Her laziness melted away her scruples, and her longing to be happy made her get as much pleasure as she could out of her troubles. She was as indulgent towards herself as towards others, and was only anxious to arrange things so that nobody was too put out. After all, you see, so long as her husband and her lover were happy, and the home went on in its regular routine and everything in it was fun and games all the livelong day, and everybody was nice and comfortable and pleased with life, there was nothing to complain about, was there? (271; 636)

The French text uses the verbs *s'accoutumer*, to accustom oneself, and *s'habituer*, to inure oneself to, to describe Gervaise's posture; the reflexive form implies that she is doing this to herself.

Her attitude toward food and, later, toward drink is the expression of her softness to herself. Eating is not only a form of self-indulgence but also a way of finding comfort and security in an environment where hunger is by no means always stilled. In one of her imaginative perceptions of the house on the day she moves in, Gervaise feels at once "joy at being at last on the point of achieving her ambition and fear of not succeeding and being crushed in this great struggle against starvation she could sense gasping for breath all round her" (136; 493). The provision of adequate and nourishing food for the family has always been one of women's primary responsibilities, and it is a duty that Gervaise takes seriously. Even when she is in labor with Nana, she insists on preparing dinner for her husband. In this instance, food is a means of expressing affection, just as later at the extravagant birthday feast an abundance of fancy dishes is a sign of prosperity.

As Gervaise's life changes, so does the function of food. Once she is established in her business, she relents occasionally in her ambitious briskness to revel in eating:

> She was getting on for twenty-eight and had put on a bit of flesh. Her fine features were taking on a certain chubbiness and her movements the slowness of contentment. Nowadays she would sometimes dawdle on the edge of a chair while waiting for an iron to heat, with a vague smile on her round, jolly face, for she was getting fond of her food, everyone agreed; but it wasn't a bad fault, quite the reverse. When you can earn enough to treat yourself to little luxuries, you would be silly to live on potato-peelings, wouldn't you? (144; 501–2)

The encouragement that Gervaise gets for her eating habits is rather interesting in this context. Eating, even somewhat excessively, is not considered a fault for two reasons: it is preferable to the drinking that is the scourge of the neighborhood, and it is also thought to be healthy to carry some fat at a time when thinness, especially in a young woman, denoted the threat of tuberculosis. From this small beginning as an earned reward for her achievements, Gervaise's gluttony gradually assumes sinister proportions as it becomes embroiled with her growing anxieties. She comes back to food as an outlet to displace other worries: "She was putting on flesh and giving in to all the little self-indulgences that go with an expanding waistline, and no longer had the strength of mind to worry about the future" (178; 538). It quickly becomes obvious that food offers Gervaise an escape, a consolation, a compensation. Her celebratory binges on every conceivable occasion reveal her dependence on food to fulfil psychological and sensual needs no longer met by Coupeau as he himself turns more and more to drink. She is driven further along this ruinous road by Virginie, who "was all for Gervaise filling herself with tidbits," and who rationalizes, "When you've got a man who drinks it all away it's only sensible, isn't it, not to let the whole caboodle be washed away in booze, but to fill your own stomach first. Since the money vanished anyway, you might just as well give it to the butcher as to the publican" (197; 558). Here again the destructive impact of the environment on Gervaise is plainly to be seen. Addicted to eating, she seizes on Virginie's excuses to let herself go further. The French word *s'abandonner*, meaning to abandon oneself to, to give oneself up to, is frequently applied to Gervaise; significantly, it is another of those reflexive verbs, like *s'accoutumer* and *s'habituer*, that show Gervaise doing bad things to herself.

Despite the self-justifications, she has some degree of bad conscience, for she feels ashamed of her overeating before Goujet. Yet she cannot stop her cult of food, which reaches its apogee in her birthday feast, when the table is set up in the middle of her shop like a shrine. The more Gervaise loses control of her life, the more she uses food as a drug to alleviate her pain and to avoid facing a confusion she knows she can no longer right. Each problem, as it were, feeds the other: as she becomes negligent, her workmanship declines and she loses customers, so that her economic situation deteriorates rapidly, especially with Lantier to provide for as well as her husband. "Her peace and quiet came first, the rest could go to hell. She had stopped worrying about her doubts which went on mounting. She was losing her sense of right and wrong—she would pay or not pay, it was just vague and she preferred not to know" (279; 644). In this wholly demoralized state, her one and only pleasure is eating three good meals per day, for this is the sole kindness to herself that she can think of. Her love of food is another manifestation of both her sensuality and her incapacity to say no. *L'Assommoir* often seems to suggest that this is less a matter of choice on her part than of entrapment in a deterministic web.

The same process can be traced in her descent into drink. Like food, it represents an escape and a consolation, more potent because of its intoxicating effects and cheaper in the form of the vile brew sold at Old Colombe's bar. Shivering with cold and haunted by hunger, Gervaise needs little more than a glass of anisette, bought for her by one of Coupeau's old buddies, to set her off. "Oh, she knew herself of old, she hadn't a ha'porth of will-power. She would only need a little push behind to send her reeling into drink. And, by the way, this anisette struck her as very good" (337; 705). The phrase "a little push behind" is a reminder of her dream, in which she sees herself as being pressured to her destruction. Already, with the first glass, she is hooked; by the second she is no longer aware of hunger and feels instead a lovely warmth throughout her body, an ease of drowsiness into which she lets her whole being slide. Everything conspires to drive her to this final self-abandonment: her heredity, the example of her environment, and the pressure of circumstances in her acute hunger. Nana's flight from home is another public degradation for Gervaise, as are the ever more menial jobs she is forced to take until she ends up cleaning Virginie's apartment. Searching for Nana in all the dance-halls, Gervaise and Coupeau treat themselves to drink the moment they have any money. Zola shows how Gervaise is caught in a vortex in which every circumstance drags her further down.

Her starvation at the end is the mirror image but also, paradoxically, the continuation of her previous gluttony. She goes on thinking obsessively in terms of food, and not only because of her tormenting hunger. When she imagines how well Nana is perhaps doing, she envisages her as being regaled with oysters. Meanwhile, her own food consists of the cheapest remnants of meat already beginning to spoil, or crusts begged from restaurants, or remnants thrown out by stores because they are bad. She now falls into the depths where mere subsistence is her main preoccupation. After thirty-six hours without food she stoops to begging from the Lorilleux, who reject her scornfully as ever. Coupeau, too, taunts her when she runs into him on his way to yet another bar, and stammers, "I'm hungry, you know. . . . I relied on you. You just find me something to eat" (392; 763). It is in fact the husband's legal obligation to support his wife, but, as L'Assommoir shows, the passion for drink overrides all normative commitments and relationships.

In her desperate hunger Gervaise turns to what has traditionally been a woman's last resort: to sell her body. She wanders the cold, dark streets, almost like a sleepwalker, occasionally recognizing a building such as the old Hotel Boncoeur, but often lost and dazed in the reconstructed parts of her district. She sees other women plying their trade and tries to imitate them, forgetting "herself in the frenzy of the chase, relentlessly pursuing the meal that was ever eluding her empty stomach" (398; 770).

> All round silent, shadowy women were moving to and fro with the strictly regular pacing up and down of animals in a cage. They emerged slowly like ghosts from the darkness, passed into the light of a gaslamp which showed up their pallid features and then faded into the shadows again, swinging the bit of white petticoat showing below their skirt, away back into the provocative mystery of the darkness. Some men let themselves be stopped, stood talking just for a lark, and then went on again, laughing. Others discreetly moved along, keeping unobtrusively about ten yards behind a woman. Murmured conversations could be heard, quarrels in voices kept low, or furious haggling which suddenly relapsed into heavy silence. Wherever she went Gervaise saw these women on sentry-go in the night, as if women were planted all along the outer boulevards. She always found one twenty paces away from another, in a line stretching on for ever, guarding Paris. Furious at being scorned, she changed her pitch and moved on from the Chaussée de Clignancourt to the Grande Rue de la Chapelle. (398–99; 770–71).

Here, as on the occasion when Gervaise tries to meet Coupeau coming out of work before he takes all his money to the bar, she finds many other women doing the same thing. The reduplication of Gervaise in a cohort of similar women suggests how typical her life is. She has no choice at this point but to resort to prostitution in an attempt to feed herself.

Gervaise is so derelict and so grotesque, as she realizes from glimpsing her own shadow, that she is unable to sell herself. Only two men stop: the first is Old Bru, himself begging a crust, which Gervaise used so generously to give him, while the second is none other than

Goujet. He takes her in, embraces her, warms her by the stove, and gives her a meal:

> She was quite inarticulate, at a loss for words. She took up the fork, but was shaking so much that she dropped it again. Her gnawing hunger made her head bob up and down like an old woman's. She had to pick the stuff up with her fingers. As she stuffed the first potato into her mouth she burst into tears. Great drops rolled down her cheeks and fell on her bread, but she went on eating, greedily devouring bread soaked in her own tears, breathing hard, her chin twitching. Goujet insisted on her drinking something so that she would not choke, and her glass rattled against her teeth.
>
> "More bread?" he asked softly.
>
> She just cried—said no—said yes—couldn't say. Oh Lord, how good and how sad it is to eat when you're starving! (403; 776)

It is a poignant scene, a kind of last supper for Gervaise, in which the offering of food is a gesture of love. It also carries echoes of the earlier episode when Gervaise had gone to see Goujet at his workplace, and had come out feeling nourished: "At twilight, on her way here along the wet pavement, she had had a vague want, like a desire to eat something nice, and now she was satisfied, as though Goldie's hammer-blows had fed her" (175; 534). The implication is that Gervaise turns to food as a substitute for love, and that there is nobody and nothing in this social system to sustain her. The lack of anyone to show kindness to her drives her to do so herself, but in a mistaken self-indulgent manner, prompted by fear of the hunger she sees around her.

In the end, Gervaise's fears prove justified. The exact cause of her death never becomes clear. The Lorilleux, spiteful to the end, maintain that she had died of "slatterliness" (422; 796); the French term, *avach-issement*, is the same word that was used when the Coupeaus flopped down to kiss on the dirty laundry. Other characters mention the cold and the heat, but the narrator adds that "the truth was that she died of poverty, from the filth and exhaustion of her wasted life" (422; 796), in which chronic malnourishment must have been a contributing factor. The neglect and ostracism of which she has been a victim is ghoulishly demonstrated by the fact that she is discovered in her hole only after several days, "turning green already" (422; 796).

Although she is not conscious of making choices, and generally doesn't have much choice, Gervaise does not deny at least some measure of responsibility for her life. She sees death as "dragging her to the end along the wretched path she had made for herself" (422; 796). Again there is the force of the reflexive verb in French, which conveys the participation of a subject in the action, the idea of doing something to oneself. It is hard to tell, however, how much importance to attach to these musings of a dying woman.

Mostly Gervaise doesn't think much about her life, and when she does, she is rather fatalistic. At times she puts the blame onto bad luck, claiming that it has always dogged her. But this is not the case. Zola is careful to allot her a balance of good and bad fortune. As an abandoned woman with two children, no money, and a limp, she is most fortunate to marry Coupeau. The support she is given by Goujet both morally through his friendship and financially through the loan to start her business is another stroke of good luck. Coupeau's accident, on the other hand, is decidedly bad luck, but surely of a kind to be reckoned with in his trade. The real misfortune stems from Coupeau's deterioration after the accident, and Gervaise undoubtedly, though unwittingly, promotes it. To ascribe her downfall primarily to chance would be to distort and simplify, for she encounters her fair share of good and bad luck.

The dark sense of fatality that hangs like a pall over *L'Assommoir* derives not from Gervaise's particularly bad fortune. Quite the contrary, if her adversities could be attributed to a singularly evil constellation of chance events, it would be almost comforting insofar as she could be regarded as an exception. It is the ordinariness of her situation that makes it so unpalatable; her lot is not uncommon for a woman of her time, place, and class. She does not have much choice, so that the outcome seems inevitable, even if she herself contributes to it through her easygoing attitude to others and to herself. Her kindness and softness are her most endearing qualities. But in the context of her harsh environment of self-interest, these positive qualities become negatives when she cannot stand firm, cannot resist or protect herself from the malevolent pressures exerted on her by her surroundings. She does not understand what happens to her. Only we readers can gradually discern the destructive patterns of interaction between this essentially decent, honest, hardworking woman and her corrupting environment. Her compliance makes her, tragically, participate in her downfall.

Chapter 7

Imagination

Toward the beginning of the last chapter of *L'Assommoir* Gervaise, in response to a letter from the hospital, makes a trip across Paris to the asylum Saint-Anne to visit Coupeau, who has been sent there after his most recent drinking spree. As she goes up the stairs, she hears "yells that made her blood run cold," and is told that the "singing" comes from her husband, who has been yelling and dancing for two whole days. Suddenly she catches sight of him:

> Oh God, what a sight! She was petrified. The cell was padded from floor to ceiling; there were two mats on the floor, one on top of the other, and in one corner a mattress and bolster, and that was all. And there Coupeau was dancing and yelling. A proper shit-bag, with his smock in tatters and his limbs beating the air, but not a funny shit-bag at all, oh no, a shit-bag whose appalling jigging made your hair stand on end. He seemed to be putting on an act as a dying duck. Christ, what a one-man show! He charged into the window, backed away from it beating time with his arms and shaking his hands as though he wanted to make them fly off and hit somebody in the face. You sometimes see comedians in the music-halls taking this off, but they imitate it so badly—you should see

the genuine drunkard's rigadoon if you want to know how smashing it looks when done properly. The song is quite stylish too, a non-stop carnival bawling, and with mouth wide open pouring forth the same hoarse trombone notes for hours and hours. Coupeau's noise was like the howling of an animal with a crushed foot. Let the orchestra strike up, swing your partners round! (409; 782)

This is a description of a patient in the grip of acute delirium tremens. Zola had read about the symptomatology and treatment in Dr. Valentin Magnan's treatise on alcoholism, which is the obvious source of this passage. Although the picture is medically accurate, its descriptive manner is anything but clinical. Coupeau is seen through the eyes of Gervaise; the account is in indirect discourse, through the prism of her mind, and it is cast in her language with all its colloquialisms, slang, and vulgarities. The carnival atmosphere evoked by the phrase "a one-man show," by the comparison to "comedians in the music-halls," and by the invocation "Let the orchestra strike up, swing your partners round!" is in ironic contrast to the grim scene of Coupeau's death-dance. It can be taken as an expression of Gervaise's black humor as well as of her backing away from him in despair. Through the mode of presentation the underlying documentary material is assimilated into the fabric of the novel, and used in an ingenious way to produce a vivid scene. The reader learns what Gervaise sees, and only indirectly what is in Magnan's textbook, which has been transformed by Zola's creative imagination.

The incident has a sequel a couple of pages later when Gervaise tries to convey to the neighbors what she has witnessed:

The ladies rolled about with mirth because all the same it did seem funny, although very sad, of course. Then, as they didn't quite get the picture, Gervaise moved everybody back, asked for floor-space and there, in the middle of the lodge, while the others looked on, she did Coupeau, bawling, jumping, flailing about with her arms and making horrible grimaces. Yes, honestly, it was just like that! The others goggled: surely it wasn't possible! A man couldn't have lasted three hours carrying on like that. Well, she swore by everything most sacred that Coupeau had been on the go since the day

98

before, thirty-six hours already. They could go and see for themselves if they didn't believe her. (411; 784)

Gervaise's imitation of Coupeau is sheer inventiveness on Zola's part.
It not only makes her a grotesque accomplice to her husband's degeneration, but also gives an eerie foreshadowing of her own fate, since
she herself is rapidly falling into alcoholism by then. In her final days,
as she loses control of her mind, her imitation of Coupeau becomes a
repetitive, almost involuntary act which suggests her adoption of his
role:

> From that day on Gervaise often wandered a bit in her mind, and
> one of the sights of the building was to see her do Coupeau. No
> need to press her now, she did her act free, gratis and for nothing,
> shaking her hands and feet and uttering little involuntary squeals.
> Presumably she had picked that up at Sainte-Anne through too
> much looking at her husband. But she never had any luck, and she
> didn't die of it as he had. It didn't go beyond ape-like grimaces
> which made urchins in the street throw cabbage-stumps at her.
> (421–22; 795)

Minor though this sequences of scenes may be in the totality of a long
novel, it is important because it shows Zola's extraordinary capacity
for the imaginative development of information he has culled from
extraneous authorities. His exuberant elaboration of Magnan's findings reveals just how much *L'Assommoir* owes to his artistic creativity.

Zola's own characterization of his writing processes, in a letter of
22 March 1885 to one of his disciples, Henry Céard, is perhaps the
most graphically telling: "I have a hypertrophy of the true detail, the
leap into the stars on the springboard of exact observation. Truth rises
as on wings into the symbolical." This catches very perceptively the
delicate equilibrium in Zola's novels between documentation and
imagination. Observation and documentation are vital facets of his
method, but imagination is at its heart. The seed of the idea for each
novel is essentially a product of the imagination, and so is the pattern
in which the collected materials are woven into the texture of the fic-

tion. The transposition of the medical report of delirium tremens into Coupeau's antics as seen by Gervaise and then into her imitation of him, first deliberately for an audience and afterward as a kind of compulsion, is an outstanding illustration of the crucial input of Zola's imagination.

The same process, this heightening and transfiguration of the actual, is apparent in the evocation of various locations which Zola visited: the bar, the forge, the laundry, and the tenement house. In each case the concrete details are illumined by a vision that transcends facticity. Often machines are personified as monsters that pose a threat to the people who come into contact with them. The steam engine, for example, in the washing establishment in the opening chapter "chuffed and snorted away without respite, and its dancing flywheel seemed to be regulating the outrageous din" (34; 387) as if it were in supreme control of all the women's activity, as indeed it is, for without hot water no washing could be done. As in other instances throughout *L'Assommoir*, the focalization is through Gervaise's eyes. Since she is new, she is far more aware of the insistent, noisy presence of the machine. "The vibration and snorting of the steam engine went on and on, without rest or pause, and seemed to emerge louder and louder until it filled the immense hall. But not one of the women noticed it, for it was like the very breathing of the washhouse, a fiery breath blowing the eternal floating mist upwards to collect among the rafters. The heat was becoming unbearable; the rays of light, striking in through the high windows to the left, turned the steamy vapour into opalescent streaks of the softest rosy-grey and grey-blue" (37–38; 391).

For a third time toward the end of the chapter there is mention of the machine turning its flywheel "puffing and blowing and making the whole place vibrate with the ceaseless plunging of its steel arms" (48; 402). The sense of menace, of the power of a ruthless, inexorable mechanism, is very palpable to Gervaise and through her to the reader. The cumulative impact on the three similar references to the steam engine within a short space reinforces the effect. What is so distinctive about *L'Assommoir*, as this example shows, is the combination of so much specific, realistic information with imaginative animation. The scene in the washing establishment gives an excellent insight into the working conditions of laundresses in the mid-nineteenth century. But at the same time, as if by a leap of Zola's imagination, it turns the work area into a surreal, almost fantastic landscape under the domination of a monster.

The forge and the still are handled in the same way. At the bolt and rivet factory the viewpoint is again Gervaise's as she visits Goujet and sees all the equipment. He tries to explain the manufacturing procedures to her. But she is so dazzled, literally and figuratively, and so full of dread that all she registers are machines that are like fiends: "The huge shed was throbbing with the vibration of the machines, and lurking shadows were streaked with red flames. . . . He went first and she followed through the deafening row in which all sorts of noises combined their hissing and roaring, amidst clouds of smoke peopled with weird shapes—black humans rushing about, machines waving their arms, she couldn't tell t'other from which" (176; 535). In an environment in which human beings are reduced to objects or mechanisms working out their predetermined course, machines are brought to life as the controlling agents. This reversal of roles between humans and machines, with the latter assuming authority over the former, is a repeated and alarming element in *L'Assommoir*. It points to the dehumanization of both men and women in a brutal environment. The preeminence of the machine also carries a political undercurrent: industrialization was replacing workers with machines in order to cut costs and increase productivity. While this was to the profit of the capitalist bourgeoisie, it was much to the detriment of the working class, who suffered wage cuts (as does Goujet) or became unemployed and pauperized. Although Gervaise herself may not fully grasp these economic problems, her dread of the machines at the forge and her sense of disorientation are a personal resonance of a deep and widespread unease at changes underway at the time. Like the rebuilding of Paris, the growing supremacy of machines, by defamiliarizing a traditional landscape, was alienating longtime inhabitants. Gervaise's visit to the factory is an imaginative, indirect way of adumbrating this complex of dilemmas.

The most sinister of the machines that Gervaise encounters is the distilling apparatus at the back of Old Colombe's bar. She is curious about it, and fascinated by it, but also instantly aware of its innate malevolence. "The still, with its weirdly shaped receptacles and endless coils of piping, looked dour and forbidding; no steam was coming out of it, but there was a scarcely perceptible inner breathing or subterranean rumble. It was like some black and midnight deed being done in broad daylight by some morose but powerful and silent worker" (57; 411). The "powerful and silent worker" is later identified by Gervaise as the poisoner of the whole neighborhood. In a series of increasingly terrifying visions, as she sits in the bar, she perceives the machine in a variety of destructive guises:

> Then suddenly she became conscious of an even more disquieting sensation behind her back. She turned round and saw the still, the drink-machine working away in the little glassed-in yard with the deep rumblings of its devil's kitchen. At night-time the copper containers looked even more sinister, their round bellies catching just a star of red light, and the shadow cast by the machine on the wall behind suggested obscene shapes, figures with tails, monsters opening their jaws to devour the whole world. (336; 704)

Sensing the spell that the still has cast over her, she envisages it as a wicked magician. "Her eyes swivelled round towards the drink-machine behind her. That blessed boiler, round as the belly of a tinker's fat wife, with its snout poking and twisting, sent a cold shiver down her back in which fear was mingled with desire. It was like the metallic entrails of some sorceress distilling drop by drop the fire that burned within her" (338; 706). Later it is "some noxious beast," and as it moves, she feels "its brass claws seizing her, while the stream was now flowing right through her body" (339; 707).

These hallucinations result, in part at least, from Gervaise's chronic intoxication as she, too, drifts into alcoholism. But beyond that they are the inventions of Zola's imagination as he devises images to make us understand Gervaise's life. So at her last glimpse of Old Colombe's bar, as she wanders the streets in search of food, it is "lit up like a cathedral for High Mass and, for Christ's sake, it really was like a service, for the blokes inside were chanting away like choristers, in their stalls, with cheeks blown up and rounded paunch" (397; 769). The bar is a symbol of the religion of alcohol that reigns in the area. The way in which it is presented through the course of *L'Assommoir* illustrates well how Zola moves from concrete, detailed description to the visionary and symbolical. The still is a specific, peculiar mechanism, but it also becomes a cipher for the degeneracy of the district.

The central objective correlative of Gervaise's life is the tenement house, which has already been discussed in the previous chapter. It changes not just as she gets to know it more intimately as an inhabitant, but above all in reflection of her own hopes and despondencies. From the beginning it has a decidedly menacing air, partly because of its overwhelming size. Many of the phrases used to describe it have negative associations or evoke fear: it is "colossal"; "the black shutters" give "the huge wall-space a look of utter desolation"; its silhouette is a "vast cube," overshadowing all the neighboring lower houses and towering over the rooftops; its cement is "decaying and flaking away in the rain"; its sides are "bare as prison walls" and its "toothing-stones like decaying jaws snapping in the void" (59; 414). As she walks into the courtyard, she notices the "filth," the "miserable poverty," and the "grime" (60; 414–15). She feels "overwhelmed by the enormity of the place . . . as though she were in the middle of some living organism, in the very heart of the city, fascinated by the building as if she were confronted by some gigantic human being" (60; 415). The building is a challenge to Gervaise; in its enormousness and with its jaws it is personified as a "living organism" and a "gigantic human being." In many respects the house is the replica of the city to which Gervaise has come—immense and daunting, yet also exciting. The water coming out of the dye-works that day is pale pink, and it arouses in Gervaise the dream of a window-box with scarlet runners (61; 416).

As she leaves after that first visit (to the Lorilleux), the effluent from the dye-works is "blue, a deep azure like a summer sky, in which the concierge's little lamp made twinkling stars" (76; 43). That is a pleasing picture, with blue standing for hope. But Coupeau calls to her to mind how she steps, and she herself feels "as though the whole building was on top of her, its chill mass crushing her shoulders" (76; 432). This dualism is characteristic of Gervaise's shifting images of the house; on the one hand, it repeatedly frightens her, while at the same time it tempts her. She wants to live there, although she watches others being mercilessly evicted for arrears in rent. Her attraction to the house summarizes her desire to participate in the life of the city despite the dangers she recognizes in it. When she reaches the sixth floor, she looks down from the top of the stairs over the railings in curiosity, and sees "the gas-jet on the ground floor that looked like a star at the bottom of the narrow, six-storey well, and all the smells and gigantic roaring life of the building rose up at her in a single breath as from a furnace and hit her frightened face as it hung poised over the abyss" (68; 423). The "roaring life" and "the abyss" are the twin aspects of the house. Both are the outcome of Gervaise's mind: the house is always as seen by her, and it functions as a kind of screen onto which she projects her moods.

Like the bar, the still, the washing establishment, and the factory, the house has its source in a model that Zola had observed. In the novel, however, he makes the character do the looking, so that the reader comes to see *her* reality through her eyes. The house that actually existed in transfigured into the house of the fiction through the mediation of Zola's imagination as well as the imagination with which he endows Gervaise. A fictive world is created that is parallel to the historical reality.

The role of the house as a mirror to Gervaise's predicaments becomes very apparent as she drops to abject poverty. She hears the misery in the house. "To pay the rent they would have sold their bodies. It was rent day which emptied the cupboard and the stove and which called forth one great lamentation from the whole building. Weeping could be heard on all floors, a song of woe moaning along the passages and stairs. If every home had somebody dead in it there could not have been more dreadful organ music. A real day of judgement, the end of all things, life unliveable, the crushing doom of the poor" (317; 683).

Her own hunger is echoed and intensified by its epidemic prevalence in her part of the house:

> In this existence embittered by poverty Gervaise's sufferings were made worse by the agonies of hunger she sensed going on all round her. This part of the building was the paupers' corner in which three or four families seemed to have agreed to go without food some days. The doors might well open, but they didn't often let out any smells of cooking. All along the passages there reigned the silence of the dying, and the very walls sounded hollow like empty stomachs. Now and again some shindy could be heard, women crying, starving children whimpering or families tearing each other to pieces to try to forget their hunger. A universal cramp in the jaw seemed to set all these famished mouths gaping, and chests went hollow merely through having to breathe the air in which not even a gnat could live for want of food. (319; 685–86)

As always, it is Gervaise's subjective perception that is recorded here and that forms the reality of the novel. Things and situations are illumined in the light cast by her imagination. While she lacks education and knowledge of the world, she undoubtedly has an acute sensibility, an innate susceptibility to the nuances of her environment. Her openness to the surrounding atmosphere—in this case of corruption—together with her easygoing disposition, makes her a ready victim, but also an apt focal figure for a novel of the dimension of *L'Assommoir*.

The interaction between Gervaise and the house is brought out one last time in a revealing passage when she returns after the meal Goujet has given her:

> The building was pitch dark and she went in as though into mourning for herself. At this hour of the night the gaping, tumbledown porch looked like jaws opening to swallow her up. To think that so long ago she had aspired to live in a corner of this great bare barrack. Her ears must have been stopped that she couldn't hear the awful hymn of despair being sung behind those walls! From the very first day that she had set foot in the place she had been going downhill. It must bring ill-luck to be piled one on top of another in

these miserable great working-class tenements in which penury was infectious, like the cholera. That night the whole lot of them seemed dead, except for the sound of the Boches snoring to the right, while to the left Lantier and Virginie were purring away like cats, not asleep, but cosy and warm with eyes closed. The courtyard looked just like a cemetery, with the snow making a pale square and the lofty walls rising up livid grey, with never a light, like ancient ruins, and not even a sigh could be heard—it was like a whole village that had died of cold and hunger and was buried. She had to step over a black stream, the outlet from the dyeworks, steaming as it cut out a muddy bed through the whiteness of the snow. The water was the colour of her thoughts. (405; 778)

The house here acts as an analogue and an extension of Gervaise's life, the embodiment of her current position. The black effluent from the dye-works is the symbolic incarnation of her own mourning over her failure. The thoughts of death uppermost in her mind become attributes of the house. The courtyard strikes her as a cemetery; the inhabitants seem dead and buried after perishing of cold and hunger, as she herself soon will be. The image of jaws opening up to swallow her is repeated, recalling also her opening vision of Paris as a monster which devours the workers. Gervaise's subconscious fear of death by being eaten is another of those poignant reversals that abound in *L'Assommoir*. She dies in fact of starvation, but in a wider, poetic sense she is indeed eaten up by the demands and pressures imposed on her by her environment. To some extent, therefore, Gervaise is justified in casting the house as a factor in her misfortune, though it must not be turned into a scapegoat. It is tangibly present as a physical setting with all its sights, smells, and sounds, yet it is stylized too as the lurid site of the foulness that pervades the slums and destroys people.

The role of the house is a striking instance of the multiple ways in which the text of *L'Assommoir* can be read: it is a part of the documentation, which gives the novel a sound base in the social reality of the time; it is an objectification of Gervaise's hopes and fears; and, thirdly, it is a manifestation of Zola's creative imagination in converting a commonplace tenement house of the period into a lasting, poetic symbol of human misery that haunts readers' minds long after they have finished the novel. This capacity to make an indelible impression on us by expanding our vicarious experience of life is one of the hallmarks of a masterpiece. The divergent ways of reading the house do not cancel each other out; on the contrary, they complement each other, fashioning a density of texture that makes the novel endlessly fascinating. At each successive reading, the reader's attention is caught by further layers of significance latent in the text.

The recurrence of the house at crucial points in Gervaise's life reveals two salient features of the narrative art of *L'Assommoir*: its intricate use of reiterated motifs rich in varying detail, and its orchestration of repetition and contrast as a structuring device. These two techniques merge into patterns that give not only meaning to Gervaise's biography but also shape to the novel.

The contrast between city and country is a good example. It is connected to one of the fundamental themes of *L'Assommoir*: the harmful impact of the city's liquor-laden culture, especially on those like Gervaise who are not inured to urban vices. Her relative innocence is emphasized in her fight with Virginie in the washing establishment when she cannot "answer back for she had not yet learned to use the slick Parisian backchat" (42; 395). She gradually becomes assimilated to the city; her move into the house denotes her absorption into the mainstream of its activities. But the country remains on the horizon as a healthier environment. One of Gervaise's early fantasies is of retirement to some peaceful rural spot; later she laughs bitterly at this aspiration and concludes that she will have her patch of grass in Père-Lachaise, the big Parisian cemetery. Indeed, she never actually leaves the city; her life, like that of most women at the time, is static.

Her repressed yearning for the country comes out in one of her conversations with Goujet when they walk together and come upon a piece of still-open ground:

> With downcast eyes they both picked their way along the uneven cobbles between the snorting factories. Then about two hundred yards further on, and quite mechanically, as if they knew their des-

tination, they turned to the left, still without a word, into a piece
of waste ground between a sawmill and a button factory. It was a
strip of green field still left, with some patches of grass burnt
brown; a goat tied to a stake was going round and round bleating,
and at the far end a dead tree was crumbling away in the sun.

"Really," said Gervaise, "you might think you were in the
country."

They went and sat down under the dead tree. She put her basket
by her feet. Opposite them were terraced one above the other, between clumps of miserable greenery, the rows of tall buildings in
Montmartre, painted yellow and grey, and when they raised their
eyes they saw a great stretch of sky with its glowing purity broken
only by a trail of little white clouds to the north. The bright light
dazzled them and they looked down again at the flat horizon with
the far-off, chalky line of suburbs, but especially they followed the
panting of the sawmill as it puffed jets of steam from its narrow
chimney. Its deep sighing seemed to relieve their heavy hearts. (250;
613–14)

This is an idyllic and consoling interlude for Gervaise, a respite from
the turmoil of the city slums, although this place, too, is quite desolate:
they sit on a dead tree crumbling in the sun, and the greenery is "miserable." Nevertheless, Gervaise leaves "gay and relaxed," carrying a
basket of dandelions (290; 617).

The restorative qualities of the country, in antithesis to the nox-
iousness of the city, are emphasized again when "Coupeau was taken
on for a job in the country, at Étampes, and there he was for nearly
three months without drinking and cured for a time by the country
air. People don't realize how refreshed drunkards are simply by getting
away from the air of the Paris streets which is really polluted by fumes
of wines and spirits" (307; 673). In the final wandering round the
streets, Gervaise thinks once more with longing of the country. From
the slaughterhouse, which is being demolished, she walks toward the
railroad station and hears the sound of a train. "She looked round as
if to follow the invisible engine as the noise died away. In that direc-
tion, through a gap between high buildings scattered haphazard on
both sides of the line, with their walls unplastered or painted with

colossal advertisements, and all a dirty yellow from the grime of the trains, she visualized the country, the great open sky. Oh, if she could have gone off like that, anywhere yonder, away from these dwellings of poverty and suffering! She might then have started to live again" (369; 768). The gloom of the city is often, as here, enhanced by darkness. The light open spaces of the country stand out against the blocked vistas and the absence of sunshine amidst the cramped buildings. The predominance of night scenes on the streets and the enclosure by edifices strongly suggest that the city dwellers are hemmed in.

Another major motif that crops up ubiquitously is that of food. Gervaise's personal relationship to food has already been discussed, but eating is important for the other characters too. Social occasions, such as Gervaise's wedding, her birthday, and Nana's first Communion are celebrated with gargantuan ceremonial meals to which friends and neighbors are invited. Zola's imagination excels in the voluptuous description of food. Another novel of the Rougon-Macquart series, *Le Ventre de Paris* (1873; variously translated as *Fat and Thin, The Markets of Paris, La Belle Lisa, The Flower and Market Girls of Paris, Savage Paris*) contains a famous passage, known as "the symphony of the cheeses," in which the appearance and smell of the cheese section of the main Parisian market are evoked. In *L'Assommoir* it is the birthday feast that marks the climax of gluttony and of Zola's inventiveness for small telling details: how the guests have fasted before to work up an enormous appetite, how they have to loosen their clothes, how they continue to stuff themselves merely for the sake of doing justice to the repast and of making the most of this opportunity. It is a scene that is at once funny, grotesque, and pathetic, as well as somewhat disgusting. It amply confirms Zola's self-diagnosis of his tendency to inflate true detail into hyperbole; yet despite its exaggerations, the episode does not strain credibility, given the environment, the tradition of vast meals in the nineteenth century, and the circumstances. It is at the birthday feast, early in her life, that Nana reveals her lust for pleasure in her geed for the best morsels. Later Lantier and Coupeau make the rounds of the local restaurants, and while savoring the specialities of each, they cement their alliance and squander Gervaise's money.

The second half of *L'Assommoir* reiterates the theme of food in an inverted form in the hunger and starvation resulting from penury. The preoccupation with food continues, though in a different guise, when the overeating of prosperity is replaced by the undereating of economic ruin. Gervaise's down-and-out nadir is also conveyed in terms of food when she begs on the streets alongside Old Bru, on whom she used to bestow her bounty, and when she accepts a charity meal from Goujet. In these incidents her degradation is translated into the idiom of food.

The perpetual presence of food in *L'Assommoir* can, like that of the house, be read on various levels: as an aspect of the novel's essential realism in showing the daily struggles and joys of life for the nineteenth-century working class, or simultaneously as a symbolical subtext that runs throughout the novel and allows us to chart Gervaise's rise and fall from another angle. It is a mark of Zola's consummate skill as a novelist that the social history blends so completely with the artistic imagination that brings the action and characters to life for the reader.

Zola's imagination runs riot with smells, perhaps because he himself was nearsighted and had a compensatory sensitivity to odors. *L'Assommoir* is surely one of the most pungent novels in world literature, abounding in good or bad smells. The frequent appeal to the sense of smell is part of the specificity and the sensuousness with which the environment is evoked. Persons as well as places are characterized by their odors. The incense in the church is to be expected, as is the smell of stale medications in the hospital. More unusual is the aura of tobacco—of a slovenly man who cares only for the surface— that Gervaise recognizes as emanating from Lantier's trunk. Nana, at age fifteen, already exudes the scent of a ripe woman, while Bazouge carries the distinctive fragrance of the cemetery. The pleasant smells are often associated with cooking: the aroma of the goose for the birthday feast wafts over the house and the street, and the sharpness of cooked onion permeates the stairwell. When Gervaise is starving, the smell of cabbage soup simmering on the Lorilleux's stove is tantalizing to her. Because the smell of cooking holds out the promise of physical well-being, Lantier, in his search for a more comfortable nest when Gervaise's cupboard is bare, tramps the streets "hunting for another crib where a nice smell of cooking would smooth away the wrinkles" (284; 649). In other words, he follows his nose. To avoid arousing the envy of their neighbors, the Lorilleux do their utmost to contain the smell of cooking when they make a rabbit stew. In a comic touch Zola has them hang a blanket over the door to prevent the smell from spreading.

Mostly, however, the smells in *L'Assommoir* are disagreeable: the alcoholic fumes on the streets are partnered by the fetid stink of the dirty laundry inside. The smell of other people's stained laundry is mentioned again and again, and as Gervaise grows negligent and the piles accumulate, it becomes worse. Some soiled laundry lies under her bed, and particularly in summer gives off an offensive exhalation, which is exceeded only by the stench of Coupeau's vomit.

While the smells in *L'Assommoir* are presented with great physical acuity, they also have metaphoric, moral implications. Sweet smells are linked to virtue, while nasty ones are redolent of vice. So the notation of odors, apart from their material dimension as an element of the environment, has an emblematic and ethical significance. The Goujets' apartment always has an appealing air of cleanliness, which is made to denote uprightness. Similarly, Lalie's quarters, which even in her last days are very neat and newly swept, have the welcome smell of good housekeeping. Conversely, the increasingly pestilent atmosphere in Gervaise's place is at once a symptom and a symbol of her deterioration. To Lantier, the parasite, the odor of the laundry represents the fulfillment of his dream to have others toil for him: "The smell of the workroom, these perspiring women ironing away with bare arms, the bedroom atmosphere littered with the underwear of the ladies of the neighbourhood, all combined to make the nook of his dreams, the long sought for haven of idleness and enjoyment" (245; 608). Gervaise's end as a bad smell in the passage fits in with the entire olfactory scheme of the novel. Such coalescence of the physical and the symbolical leads to a richness and density of texture that makes *L'Assommoir* a masterpiece.

The proliferation of smells in *L'Assommoir* heightens the reality of the world that Zola is portraying by allowing the reader to experience that world through another sense. Just as we can see the tenement house through Gervaise's eyes, so we can smell this environment with our noses. In this way Zola's imagination brings the reader's imagination into play too.

Another means of drawing the reader into the world of the fiction is the widespread use of slang and colloquialisms. Here again Zola is using his sources in an original, innovative manner. For the speech of the people appears not only in dialogue, when characters are actually talking to each other, but also in the narration. Zola achieves this because he so often has recourse to free indirect discourse, slipping into the mind of Gervaise and letting her tell her view of her situation in her own language. Like the use of smells, this technique fosters the reader's immersion in the fictive realm. We come to know how the rue de la Goutte d'Or looks and smells and sounds, and we do so because of the brilliance of Zola's imaginative techniques of narration.

Imagination also inspires another important subsidiary pattern of details: the frequent animal imagery. Particularly in the latter part of the novel, comparisons of people to animals abound: Gervaise, with her mounting debts, is "like a beaten cur" (279; 644); the Lorilleux are said to live "like a couple of skinny spiders" (317; 683); Lalie's father is "like a mad wolf falling upon a poor, timid and gentle kitten" (323; 689); Nana is "nicknamed the little chicken because she really had the tender flesh and freshness of a chicken" (341; 709–10); she takes "to vice like a duck to water" (351; 720—the French refers to her as "a fish"); Lantier calls her "a real little serpent! So nice, full of woman's wiles, licking you like a dog" (363; 733); Coupeau, during his death dance, seems to Gervaise to have "an animal's muzzle" (410; 783); Poisson, when he catches his wife with Lantier, is reported to behave "like a tiger" (421; 795); Gervaise, scrubbing Virginie's floor, makes "froglike movements" (364; 734). There is, moreover, an animalistic nucleus to the word most often used to describe Gervaise's decline: the reflexive verb *s'avachir* and the noun derived from it, *avachissement*. From the root *vache* (cow), *s'avachir* is a strongly derogatory word literally meaning to wear out and get out of shape, and figuratively, to let oneself go to the bad. The reiterated animal analogies in the last third of *L'Assommoir* form an effective subtext to underscore the dehumanization caused by this environment. Where machines become monsters, people become mechanisms or animals.

Recurrence is used in *L'Assommoir* not only for imagery and thematically but also as a structural device. Trips to the pawnshop, for instance, punctuate the action, becoming increasingly common during the period of decline, but stopping abruptly when there is nothing more to pawn. The state of Gervaise's laundry business is another recurrent marker of her position. From a fond dream it turns into a reality when she finds the vacant store and gets the loan from Goujet. All renovated, it causes a sensation in the district with its pale blue sign and yellow lettering, whitewashed ceiling, and fresh pale blue paint with yellow touches (138–40; 495–97). Its initial appearance signals cleanliness, wholesomeness, and hope. Gradually it becomes more and more encumbered with dirty linen waiting to be washed and giving off a nauseating odor. The deterioration in the store's upkeep and atmosphere objictifies in a tangible, visible (and smellable) way Gervaise's own degeneration:

> You would never have recognized the lovely sky-blue shop that had once been Gervaise's pride and joy. The woodwork and windows of the shopfront were now never cleaned and were splashed from top to bottom with mud from passing vehicles. In the shop window, hanging on the brass rod, were three grey rags that had belonged to customers who had died in hospital. And inside it was even more depressing: the damp from drying washing had loosened the paper on the ceiling, and the Pompadour chintz hung in shreds like cobwebs heavy with dust; in its corner the broken stove, with holes in made by the poker, looked like some old iron in a junk-shop; the work-table looked as if it had been used for meals by a whole garrison, stained with coffee and wine, plastered with jam and greasy with the remains of Monday blowouts. Add to all that a reek of stale starch and a stench made up of mildew, burnt fat and dirt. (278–79; 643–44)

By referring back to the shop's pristine start and contrasting that with its present dilapidation, Zola is obliquely showing Gervaise's demoralization. The full force of his imaginative invention comes to the fore when the store is taken over by Virginie, who has it done up spanking new again as a candy shop. Once more the motif of food surfaces, with the woman as nurturer and the man as devourer. Lantier will eat up Virginie's business, as he has Gervaise's. The cyclical pattern in the succession of the stores suggests the generality of the woman's lot in this environment. Similarly, Nana's taking possession of Grandma Coupeau's big bed the moment the old woman dies represents the passage of the generations, the natural continuities in the ascent of the young, healthy, and self-seeking. The significance of these episodes reaches beyond the immediate situations; by parallels and echoes the entire novel is compositionally intertwined, each incident acting as a reflective comment on the others.

Repetition functions as a structuring principle too, sometimes even in a symmetrical shape. The close of L'Assommoir is an inverted replay of the opening: now Gervaise sees the workmen returning home after a day's work just as she had watched them walking to work at the outset. The same word, "herd" (394; 765) is used of the workers, and Gervaise for one last time passes the Hotel Boncoeur, the hospital, the house, and the slaughterhouse. The reiteration serves to bring out the contrast between the youthful, attractive woman new to the city and the exhausted old hag into which her experiences have transformed her.

These cyclical repetitions intersect with the linear progression of L'Assommoir. The novel's plot is formed by the biography of Gervaise from her arrival in Paris to her death nineteen years later. The vicissitudes of her life create the up-and-down pattern of the novel. It starts in an atmosphere of anxiety at a fairly low ebb for her as she sits up all night waiting for Lantier to come back to their temporary home. The first chapter reaches its turning point in the brusque announcement "Daddy's gone" (40; 393), which augurs a dramatic decline in Gervaise's fortune. The great pitched battle with Virginie brings the exposition to an exciting climax before dropping back to the apprehensive mood of the opening in Gervaise's gloomy reflections on her future. The second chapter, by contrast, begins three weeks later on an upbeat note when Gervaise meets Coupeau for a drink. With his attentions to her, her life turns a corner; its "line" is a steadily rising one through the courtship in chapter 2, the wedding in chapter 3, and the first four years of their marriage, a phase of hard work, prosperity, and saving recorded in chapter 4. Coupeau's accident is undoubtedly another downturn for Gervaise, but thanks to Goujet's loan it appears to be only a temporary setback. In chapters 5 through 7 the picture is complicated by conflicting countercurrents. On the surface Gervaise's ascent is unchecked, with the move into her store in chapter 5, her success in business, the respect she earns in the district, and her generous hospitality in chapter 7. However, there are also ominous portents to suggest the dangers already implicit in her situation: Coupeau's idleness and his inclination to drink, her own over-indulgence in food, the lurking shadow of Lantier, and the money problems resulting from her extravagance. These diverse negative elements all coalesce in chapter 7, the birthday feast, where Gervaise reaches the zenith of her affluence and regard in the neighborhood, but which also creates the conditions for her downfall through Lantier's return into the family's orbit.

The structure of *L'Assommoir* is perfectly symmetrical, with six chapters leading up to the central one of the birthday feast and a further six following it to chronicle Gervaise's decline. After the exuberance of the party, the picture grows progressively more sombre with each chapter as Gervaise rapidly goes downhill. The earlier tension at the prospect of a further encounter with Lantier yields to resignation as she lets things happen without putting up much resistance. Bad events pile up on her: the burden, financial and moral, of the ménage à trois in chapter 8 is followed by the death of Grandma Coupeau, the ruin of her business, and the break with Goujet in chapter 9. The move out of the store into cramped, dingy quarters in chapter 10, which marks a further stage in Gervaise's descent, again reveals the symmetry of the novel's construction as it balances the move into the store in chapter 5. The last four chapters portray the unmitigated disasters that beset Gervaise: poverty, hunger, and alcohol in chapter 10, the humiliation of menial jobs and the aggravation of Nana's escapades in chapter 11, the unsuccessful attempts at begging and prostitution in chapter 12, and Coupeau's death from alcoholism and her own ignominious demise in chapter 13. While her rise is slow and faltering, her fall is charged with an unrelenting impetus.

The downward movement that governs the entire shape of *L'Assommoir* is reflected in most of its individual chapters. They tend to start in relative optimism with some fresh enterprise or segment in Gervaise's life only to end in a renewed outburst of doubt or despair. Even the birthday celebration in chapter 7 conforms to this pattern. It begins in elegant splendor with a beautifully set table, gifts of flowers, the guests dressed up, and, of course, a profusion of rich food and wine; but it closes in the squalid disarray of drunkenness and over-eating, the context of the demoralization that permits the return of Lantier. In the final paragraph of that chapter Zola's agile imagination is very much in evidence: "Madame Lerat had refused to walk home to the Batignolles at that hour, and so they took one mattress off the bed and put it down in a corner of the shop after shifting the table. And there she slept all among the remains of the dinner. All night long, while the Coupeaus were flat out, sleeping off the effects of the party, a neighbour's cat, who had taken advantage of an open window, crunched the bones of the goose and laid it finally to rest with the tiny sound of its sharp little teeth" (232; 595). The human participants' abrupt slump into sleep in the middle of the debris of the meal is contrasted with the cat's alert activity. Again, the implication is that the human beings have become animalistic in their exclusive pursuit of physical desires, while the goose seems to acquire dignity through the idea of being "laid . . . finally to rest," like a person. The vivid auditory detail of "the tiny sound of [the cat's] sharp little teeth" is a brilliant invention to round off this whole noisy, grotesque episode.

This is not an isolated example. Zola has a remarkable aptitude for devising striking conclusions to the chapters in brief scenes that summarize the current situation and act as unspoken commentary on the action. Often the realizations that crystallize for the protagonists and for the reader in these closing vignettes have a stunning effect, so that the chapters are made to end on a resounding bang. In the first chapter, for example, it is Gervaise's despondent vision of her future life, which "was going to live itself out in this place, between a slaughterhouse and a hospital" (49; 403). Her early awareness of her entrapment between two theaters of death—and of her own powerlessness—forms a haunting finale to the exposition. An intensified repetition of the same sense of imprisonment occurs at the close of chapter 6, when Gervaise again harbors gloomy thoughts after suddenly recognizing the extent of Coupeau's alcoholism:

> Coupeau was actually crossing the street. He nearly smashed a pane of glass with his shoulder as he lurched for the door. He was nasty drunk, with teeth clenched and nose pinched in. Gervaise recognized at once the poison of that pub in the vitiated blood that discoloured his skin. She made as if to laugh it off and put him to bed as she did on days when the wine made him merry. But this time he shoved her aside without unclenching his teeth and raised his fist to her as he pushed past and threw himself on to the bed. He looked just like the other one, the drunk snoring up there, worn out with beating his wife. And a chill came over her as she thought of the men in her life—her husband, Goujet, Lantier—her heart was torn asunder and she despaired of ever being happy again. (196–97; 557)

The mirror image of this scene comes at the end of chapter 10, where Gervaise is seen by Lalie: "But catching sight of Gervaise's fuddled expression she drew back and trembled. She knew that smell of spirits, those bleary eyes, that contorted mouth. Gervaise staggered on without a word, and the child stood at her door watching her with her dark eyes, silent and solemn" (340; 708).

On two occasions, the closing focus is on Nana, showing her response to the events in her family. At the end of chapter 8, she catches a glimpse of "her father wallowing in his own vomit" and sees her mother's petticoat "disappear into the other man's room opposite. She concentrated attentively, and the child's vicious eyes, staring wide, were lit up with a lubricious curiosity" (268; 633). The concluding sentence of chapter 9 tells how "that night she slept bloody well, in the lovely tickly warmth of the feather bed" (305; 671) to which she succeeds on Grandma Coupeau's death. The endings of the last three chapters chart the ultimate stages of Gervaise's disintegration. At the close of chapter 11 Coupeau callously urges her to try prostitution: "Look, my dear, I'm not stopping you. You're still not too bad when you're cleaned up. . . . You know the saying: no saucepan's too old to find a lid. Well, why not, if it puts butter on our bread?" (378; 748). Bazouge, the grave-digger, is kinder to her at the end of chapter 12, refusing her plea to him to take her away with wry humor. "But, bless you, there's one little operation that has to be done first, you know— *kkkk*" (407; 780). This is his way of describing, audibly, the process of dying that has to precede burial. The last words of the novel are an inverted echo of this rejection, in Bazouge's final acceptance of her for burial: "Listen, dear . . . you know . . . it's me, Bibi-la-Gaieté, known as the ladies' comforter. . . . There, there, you're all right now. Night-night, my lovely!" (423; 796). He lays her in the coffin like a loving father. This tender care of Gervaise after her death is an ironic comment on the environment that has brutalized her in her lifetime. So *L'Assommoir* ends overtly on a quiescent, conciliatory note, yet not without a covert hint of social criticism. Each of the chapter closures is designed to startle readers and make them reflect on the events of the novel.

All these subtle interconnections between the various episodes— this web of recurrences, echoes, contrasts, and repetitions—become increasingly apparent the more closely the text is studied. It is a measure of Zola's mature and imaginative art as a novelist that each incident in *L'Assommoir,* however minor, makes a significant contribution to the whole, like pieces fitting into a mosaic. With each re-reading its dense texture yields new understanding of the imagination that has transformed documentation and experience into a compelling and lasting work of art. After finishing the novel, it is rewarding to return to the opening chapter in order to see how superbly this novel is arranged from the first word on.

The opening chapter of *L'Assommoir* pays immediate testimony to the force of Zola's imagination and the excellence of the novel's design, although its many disparate elements can be appreciated only after the entire novel has been read. It is in a rereading, when the plot is already known, that its inventive craftmanship can be analyzed. As exposition the chapter is a masterpiece of economy and vividness. Although it covers some twenty-five pages, its action all takes place in a single day, beginning at five A.M. when Gervaise wakes from a short sleep during her vigil; it follows her through a day of cleaning, housekeeping, washing, talking to neighbors, and tending to her children and her obligations. It is an ordinary day in a nineteenth-century working woman's life, yet it is also extraordinary for her since it is the day when Lantier leaves her. The very first sentence, "Gervaise had sat up until two in the morning waiting for Lantier" (23; 375), straightaway suggests trouble, thereby arousing the reader's curiosity. It also puts the spotlight unmistakably onto Gervaise from the initial word. The unity of time in the single day is matched by the limitation of place: Gervaise moves merely between her narrow temporary home and the washing establishment. The major landmarks in her district, the slaughterhouse on one side and the hospital on the other, are symbolic indicators of her confinement both physically in an area and morally in a situation of duress.

The chapter is composed of three sections: Gervaise's wait at home, her conversation with Madame Boche at the washing establishment, and her battle with Virginie. Madame Boche's questions to her as a newcomer are a clever means to provide the reader with information about Gervaise's past, her origins, and her life up to the point where the novel starts. Her present predicament after the news of Lantier's walkout is also clearly delineated in Madame Boche's concerned response. The fight with Virginie is a dramatic representation of the strife characteristic of the novel's environment as well as of the difficulties Gervaise is likely to face as an ignorant outsider. The brief coda at the end returns Gervaise to the position where she was at the beginning. The shape of the chapter is therefore circular, with Gervaise starting and finishing at home, in the meantime making a foray out into the district.

However, the end of chapter 1 differs decisively from the beginning in one respect: Gervaise has been abandoned by Lantier. The action of the novel, the story of Gervaise's struggles, has been set in motion. All three of the major figures are adroitly introduced, with a casual appearance by Coupeau as a friendly fellow tenant in the Hotel Boncoeur. The flavor of the environment is conveyed in the descriptions of the slum housing, the working conditions in the washing establishment, the financial exigency, and the animalistic savagery of the fight for survival. The use of slang also helps to plunge us right into that environment. The balance is nicely maintained between the interest in the characters and in the milieu, already adumbrating their close interdependence. The alternation between direct narration and dialogue is skillfully managed, as is the shift of viewpoint. At the beginning the narration is impersonal, as an unidentified narratorial voice observes Gervaise and tells of her actions. But by the close of the chapter the focalization is from Gervaise's perspective; Zola has moved into her mind so that the subsequent happenings are recorded as experienced by her. This change in the narrational disposition in the course of the opening chapter is as important for the novel as Lantier's disappearance is for the action. Because we as readers see with and through Gervaise, we are enabled in *L'Assommoir* to gain a lively sense of a mid-nineteenth-century working-class woman's life.

Notes and References

1. *Les Rougon-Macquart,* ed. Henri Mittérand (Paris: Gallimard, 1961), 2:1543. My translation. All subsequent French references are to this edition.

2. *L'Assommoir,* trans. Leonard W. Tancock (Harmondsworth, England, and Baltimore: Penguin Books, 1970), 21. All English references are to this edition.

3. For a list of early reviews see *Les Rougon-Macquart,* 2:1568–69.

4. Georg Lukács, "The Zola Centenary," in *Critical Essays on Émile Zola,* ed. David Baguley (Boston: G.K. Hall, 1986), 80–89.

5. Guy Robert, *Émile Zola: Principes et caractères généraux de son oeuvre.* Paris: Belles Lettres, 1952.

6. Angus Wilson, *Émile Zola: An Introductory Study of His Novels* (New York: Morrow, 1952).

7. Lionel Trilling, "In Defense of Zola," in *A Gathering of Fugitives* (Boston: Beacon Press, 1956), 12–19.

8. F. W. J. Hemmings, *Émile Zola* (London and New York: Oxford University Press, 1970), 117.

9. Harry T. Levin, *The Gates of Horn: A Study of Five French Realists* (New York: Oxford University Press, 1963), 327.

10. *L'Assommoir,* trans. Mary Neal Sherwood (Philadelphia: Peterson, 1879); *Gervaise,* trans. E. Binsse (New York: Carleton, 1879); *The "Assommoir"* (London: Vizetelly, 1884); *L'Assommoir,* trans. Arthur Symons (London; Lucretian Society, 1895); *The Dram Shop,* ed. E. Vizetelly (London: Chatto & Windus, 1987); *Drink,* trans. S. J. A. Fitzgerald (London: Greening, 1903); *The Dram Shop,* trans. Gerard Hopkins (London: Hamish Hamilton, 1951); *The Gin Palace,* trans. Buckner B. Trawick (New York: Avon, 1952); *L'Assommoir,* trans. Atwood H. Townsend (New York: New American Library, 1962); *L'Assommoir,* trans. Leonard W. Tancock (Harmondsworth, England, and Baltimore: Penguin Books, 1970).

11. "The Experimental Novel," in *Documents of Modern Literary*

Realism, ed. George J. Becker (Princeton, N.J.: Princeton University Press, 1963), 166.

12. Ibid., 168.

13. *Les Rougon-Macquart,* 2:1548.

14. Ibid., 1551.

15. Ibid., 1553.

16. Patricia E. Prestwich, *Drink and the Politics of Social Reform: Antialcoholism in France since 1870* (Palo Alto, Calif.: Society for the Promotion of Science and Scholarship, 1988), 89. I am most grateful to Susan Groag Bell for indicating this book to me.

17. *Les Rougon-Macquart,* 2:798.

18. Ibid., 5:914.

19. Becker, *Documents of Modern Literary Realism,* 160; *Les Rougon-Macquart,* 1:3.

20. *Les Rougon-Macquart,* 5:1692–1728.

21. Ibid., 5:1723.

22. Ibid., 5:1728.

23. Ibid., 5:1693.

24. Ibid., 5:1694; Zola's italics.

25. Ibid., 5:1702.

26. "The Experimental Novel," 160–61; *Les Rougon-Macquart,* 1:3.

27. "The Experimental Novel," 161; *Les Rougon-Macquart,* 1:3.

28. "The Experimental Novel," 171.

29. Levin, *The Gates of Horn,* 339.

30. *Les Rougon-Macquart,* 5:1701.

31. *Les Rougon-Macquart,* 2:1544.

Selected Bibliography

Primary Works

L'Assommoir. Translated by L. W. Tancock. Harmondsworth, England, and Baltimore: Penguin Books, 1970, 1971.

Correspondance. Edited by H. H. Bakker in association with Colette Becker. Montreal: University of Montreal Press, 1978–.

Le Roman expérimental. Paris: Fasquelle, 1913. "The Experimental Novel" translated in ed. George J. Becker, pp. 162–96, *Documents of Modern Literary Realism.* Princeton, N.J.: Princeton University Press, 1963.

Les Rougon-Macquart. Vol. 2. Edited by Henri Mittérand, pp. 373–796. Paris: Gallimard, 1971.

Secondary Works

Books

Ahnebrink, Lars. *The Beginnings of Naturalism in American Fiction.* Cambridge, Mass.: Harvard University Press, 1950. Traces Zola's impact on Hamlin Garland, Stephen Crane, and Frank Norris.

Baguley, David, ed. *Critical Essays on Émile Zola.* Boston: G.K. Hall, 1986. Includes a survey of Zola criticism in the Introduction and a large variety of provocative essays.

Becker, Colette, ed. *Les Critiques de notre temps et Zola.* Paris: Garnier, 1972. A wide-ranging collection of short essays in French on various aspects of Zola's life, works, and time.

Bernard, Marc, ed. *Zola par lui-même.* Paris: Editions du Seuil, 1952. Zola's own views about his novels.

Block, Haskell M. *Naturalistic Triptych: The Fictive and the Real in Zola, Mann, and Dreiser.* New York: Random House, 1970. Investigates the sources of *L'Assommoir* and their transformation into fiction.

Brown, Calvin S. *Repetition in Zola's Novels.* Athens: University of Georgia Press, 1952. A study of one of Zola's most important devices.

Carter, Lawson A. *Zola and the Theater.* New Haven, Conn.: Yale University Press, 1963. A study of the development of Zola's dramatic theories, his plays, librettos, and dramatic criticism. Also discusses stage adaptations of his novels.

Charlton, D. G. *Positivist Thought in France during the Second Empire 1852–1870.* Oxford: Clarendon Press, 1959. The history-of-ideas context for Zola's writings.

Deffoux, Léon. *La Publication de "L'Assommoir."* Paris: Société Française D'Éditions Littéraires et Techniques, 1931. Documents the circumstances of publication and the early critical responses.

Dubois, Jacques. *"L'Assommoir" de Zola.* Paris: Larousse, 1973. In a series on society, discourse, and ideology, offers a sociologically oriented semiotic reading of the novel.

Furst, Lilian R., and Peter N. Skrine. *Naturalism.* London and New York: Methuen, 1971, 1976. Places Zola in the context of the literary movement he led.

Grant, Elliot M. *Émile Zola.* New York: Twayne, 1966. A concise, scholarly, and readable introduction to Zola's life and works.

Hemmings, F. W. J. *The Age of Realism.* Harmondsworth, England, and Baltimore: Penguin, 1976. Wide ranging collection of essays on literary realism in England, France, Germany, Italy, Russia, Spain, and Portugal.

———. *Culture and Society in France 1848–1898.* New York: Scribner's, 1971. Interesting and illuminating introduction to the cultural and artistic life of the period.

———. *Émile Zola.* London and New York: Oxford University Press, 1970. Good basic critical introduction.

———. *The Life and Times of Émile Zola.* New York: Scribner's, 1977. Well written though somewhat romanticized biography.

King, Graham. *Garden of Zola: Émile Zola and His Novels for English Readers.* New York: Harper & Row, 1978. Despite its attractive title a superficial and inaccurate book.

Knapp, Bettina L. *Émile Zola.* New York: Ungar, 1980. A straightforward introduction.

Levin, Harry T. *The Gates of Horn: A Study of Five French Realists,* pp. 305–71. New York: Oxford University Press, 1963. A brilliant, sophisticated essay on Zola's novels.

Selected Bibliography

Massis, Henri. *Comment Émile Zola composait ses romans*. Paris: Charpentier, 1906. The genesis of *L'Assommoir* and Zola's working methods.

Max, Stéfan. *Les Métamorphoses de la grande ville dans "Les Rougon-Macquart."* Paris: Nizet, 1966. Stimulating but demanding analysis of the portrayal of the city in *The Rougon-Macquarts*.

Patterson, J. G. *A Zola Dictionary*. London: Routledge, 1912. Still a useful compendium with synopses of the plots of the Rougon-Macquart novels.

Prestwich, Patricia E. *Drink and the Politics of Social Reform: Alcoholism in France since 1870*. Palo Alto, Calif.: Society for the Promotion of Science and Scholarship, 1988. Gives fascinating insight into the alcoholic environment.

Richardson, Joanna. *Zola*. London: Weidenfeld and Nicolson, 1978. Hard-headed critical biography.

Robert, Guy. *Émile Zola: Principes et caractères généraux de son oeuvre*. Paris: Belles Lettres, 1952. Standard introduction in French to Zola's work.

Salvan, Albert J. *Zola aux Etats-Unis*. Providence, R.I.: Brown University Press, 1943. A history of Zola's literary reputation in the United States.

Turnell, Martin. *The Art of French Fiction*. Norfolk, Conn.: New Directions, 1959. Contains a chapter (pp. 91–194) on Zola, treating the development of the theme of fall and redemption, including discussion of *L'Assommoir*.

Walker, Philip. *Émile Zola*. New York: Humanities Press, 1969. A survey of Zola's life and works through selected extracts.

Wilson, Angus. *Émile Zola: An Introductory Study of His Novels*. New York: Morrow, 1952. A lively general study with Freudian insights.

Wright, Gordon. *France in Modern Times*. 3d rev. edition. New York: Norton, 1981. Excellent overview of political, social, and cultural history.

Articles

Burns, Colin. "Documentation et imagination chez Émile Zola." *Les Cahiers naturalistes* 24–25 (1963): 69–78.

Decker, Clarence R. "Zola's literary reputation in England." *Publications of the Modern Language Association of America* 49 (1934): 1140–54. Records the British reaction to Zola.

Dubois, Jacques. "Les Refuges de Gervaise: Pour un décor symbolique de *L'Assommoir*." *Les Cahiers naturalistes* 30 (1965): 105–17. Phenomenological analysis of the setting of *L'Assommoir*.

Trilling, Lionel. "In Defense of Zola." In *A Gathering of Fugitives*, pp. 12–

19. Boston: Beacon Press, 1956. A brief but important essay that empha-
sizes Zola's imaginative qualities.

Bibliographies

Baguley, David. *Bibliographie de la critique sur Émile Zola. Vol. 1: 1864–1970; Vol. 2: 1971–1980.* Toronto: University of Toronto Press, 1976, 1982. Each volume contains a large number of references in English; the bibliography continues annually in the journal *Les Cahiers naturalistes.*

Hemmings, F. W. J. *The Life and Times of Émile Zola,* pp. 97–122. London: Elek, 1956; New York: Scribner's, 1977. Reprinted in *The Present State of French Studies: A Collection of Research Reviews,* edited by Charles B. Osburn, pp. 586–623, 951–54. Metuchen, N. J.: Scarecrow Press, 1971.

Lethbridge, Robert. "Twenty Years of Zola Studies (1956–1975)." *French Studies* 31 (1977): 281–93. Follows from the Hemmings article above.

Nelson, Brian. *Émile Zola: A Selective Analytical Bibliography.* London: Grant and Cutler, 1982. Indispensable reference work—in English.

Schor, Naomi. "Zola and *la nouvelle critique.*" *L'Esprit créateur* 11 (1971): 11–20.

Index

About the Author

Lilian R. Furst is the Marcel Bataillon Professor of Comparative Literature at the University of North Carolina in Chapel Hill. She received her Ph.D. from Cambridge University and has taught at various universities in Great Britain and the United States. Her primary area of interest is nineteenth-century European literature. Her publications include *Romanticism in Perspective, Romanticism, Naturalism, Counterparts, The Contours of European Romanticism, European Romanticism: Self-Definition,* and *Fictions of Romantic Irony.* She has developed the course "Women and Work 1850–1900" that links social and intellectual history with literature and uses *L'Assommoir* as one of its examples. Dr. Furst wrote this book during her year as a fellow at the National Humanities Center in Research Triangle Park, North Carolina.